MAKE YOUR MOUTH A MINISTRY

Speak Life...

DEBORAH LEANER

Cover Photo Credit: Nick Monu/Index Stock
Cover Design: Ayannah Buford, Patricia A. Jackson & Leah Williamson
Interior Design: Patricia A. Jackson
Editor: Laura C. Jackson
Back Cover Author Photo: Sade Dennis

ISBN-13: 978-0-9816888-0-0
ISBN-10: 0-9816888-0-2

Printed in the United States of America

For Korey

My son, who showed me how speaking words that give hope can
change the state of darkness in a
person's life, in spite of what they are
going through.

"Now therefore, go, and
I will be with your mouth
and teach you
what you shall say."

Exodus 4:12

Contents

PART II

MAKING YOUR MOUTH A MINISTRY IN EVERYDAY LIFE

PART III

ENTER THE SPLENDOR OF THE TEA ROOM

PART IV

Very Special Thanks

It has taken teamwork for the elements of this book to come together. I extend these expressions from my heart:

First, I give honor to God for what He has done in my life during this season and how He has kept me. He has given me Beauty for My Ashes and given light to one of the darkest times in my life.

Tony Leaner, my awesome husband, you are my Love Line. You have demonstrated your love towards me over and over and over again. You are my champion who expresses excitement for what God is doing in my life, daily. You believe in me, stand with me and push me towards the gifts God has placed in me. Your love keeps me like a well-oiled machine. I love you.

Mother and Father, my strong tower. Your union of 54 years illustrates to me what commitment before God means. I can stand up in my marriage because yours has been a living testimony of what strength in a marriage should be.

In memory of my son, Korey Leaner, a perfect gift from God—an inspiration for this book. Long ago I realized that you were my special gift from God. And now I have surrendered the gift back to God, for I realize that only God gives and takes life for His glory.

Pastor Jenkins and First Lady Trina, my pastor and my first lady, I sincerely thank you both for your encouraging and uplifting words during my darkest hour.

Tara Perrin, a gentle and quiet spirit. You were the first person to step forward and help me decipher the thoughts that kept running through my head. You typed as I dictated those thoughts for over a year—every Thursday night.

Beauty for Ashes Magazine Team, all of you have helped me in writing this book and I thank each one of you. Tarka, who spent two weekends away from her family writing as I listened to God speak the contents of the book; Laura, who diligently edited this entire book; Pat, who gave of herself to add visual life to the words of this book, Ayannah, whose unselfishness led to the appropriate image for this cover, and Jackie, who developed the website in spite of all of the challenges she faced, I say a Big Thank YOU.

"Make Your Mouth a Ministry" Team, you have made it possible to unveil the ministry that God placed in my heart through this book. Working endless nights and weekends in excellence, you have developed ambassadors for the "circle of influence" gatherings and prepared the 'Speak Life' challenges. Your contributions will make a difference in the lives of humanity. I love you and thanks from the bottom of my heart.

The Media Team, thank you for all that you have and will do to get this "Truth" to the ends of the earth. I bless God for people like you! As God continues to raise you up remember the tea room is in you and the ministry is in your mouth.

Readers of this book, whether in a book club, as an ambassador, church ministry group, hair salons, book clubs, sorority or fraternity, social gathering, it doesn't matter, I believe that reading this book will release the latent power within your mouth to "speak life" into some of the most critical issues of life for your loved ones.

Office volunteers, Marilyn and Dionne, you keep me from falling; my heart belongs to you. Thank you.

Introduction

I wrote this book to stir up the latent power in the mouths of ordinary people who want God to use them in extraordinary ways. In this book we won't be concerned about scholarships but instead relationships. We won't be interested in ability but instead availability. Last, we'll walk intimately with Him and He will get all the glory!

Welcome to 21st century ministry: intimate, personal, collaborative, life-changing, transforming, and transparent. Ministry today requires you to give of yourself and get out of the bed, get off the pew, the couch, or the stump and get involved with family, friends, neighbors, and even strangers in a way you've never imagined. Ministry will become a part of your being; indeed, it will draw upon your experiences to help others walk through the shadows of death as you allow God to use you as a lifeline. Making your mouth a ministry requires you to align your mouth with the heartbeat of God, affirm your family and friends, cultivate a heart of humility, intercede in prayer for others, encourage yourself and others, speak the truth in love, and continually equip yourself for ministry.

To accept this call to make your mouth a ministry, you must know and understand the power of your words. We are ordinary people prepared by God to speak life into the lives of family, friends, and even strangers in an extraordinary way. This book will illustrate the pleasure, pain, and impact of your words on others. You'll learn that your words can either bring life, love, edification, and encouragement into a person's life or bring negativity, torment, death, and destruction.

Let There Be Light

The book of Genesis tells us that in the beginning, *"The earth was without form, and void; and darkness was on the face of the deep. And the Spirit of God was hovering over the face of the waters. Then God said, Let there be light: and there was light."* (Gen.1: 2-3).

This scripture reveals the power God has over darkness, assuring us that with God we have the victory over darkness and the ability to speak light into it and transcend it by the power of God's word. This scripture gives us the confidence to speak into the lives of those whose faces have been covered by darkness and expect to see the light manifested in their lives. Once you accept your assignment from God to speak a word with expectation in their lives, you, too, will witness how light evaporates darkness.

Darkness manifests itself in many ways. In the lives of family and friends, darkness comes through the spirit of depression, fear, frustration, desperation, discouragement, death, and despair--just to name a few.

When this happens, it's imperative that you're ready to speak a word into someone's life with boldness and truth. The truth, which is the word of God, will hover over the issues of life that they're faced with and separate the darkness from the light in their lives. God can use you in a powerful way if you allow Him to choose your words and make your mouth a ministry.

So many of us walk this earth daily unaware that God will call us out to use our experiences as a lifeline to someone. He calls us to speak a word of life into a dying situation. No one escapes. We'll all participate at one time or another, prepared or unprepared. This is why I had to write the book. Somewhere along your journey in life you'll need to speak with truth and boldness as a loved one's life hangs in the balance. Will you be ready or will your folks have to go through the darkness alone?

A Bridge to Your Destiny

"Make your mouth a ministry" isn't just a slogan. It's a cry for the people of God to stir up the latent power in their mouths and exercise the "Speak Life" muscle in their mouths as a bridge to the ministry that God has called each one of us to for such a time as this.

This book will challenge you to speak life as a spiritual calling, which requires intimacy with God daily as He cleans your heart and prepares you for ministry. Your Heavenly Father wants to teach you Himself (John 14:26). You must accept and embrace the calling to function in this ministry. You can't tame, control, or even bridle your tongue without the power of the Holy Spirit. My grandmother told me a long time ago that "Your mouth ain't no river, but it will surely drown you." She had seen firsthand the damage the mouth could cause if not aligned with the Holy Spirit. James 3:8 says, "But no man can tame the tongue. It is an unruly evil, full of deadly poison."

When we're aligned with the Holy Spirit, we all have the power in our mouths to encourage or serve others. Barbara Brown states in her devotional notes that we should be aware of what we speak for words are fruit of the lips. She goes on to say that we must understand that most fruit produces seeds, which in season will manifest its kind. A man who speaks positive words of health, good will, love, peace, and blessings will in return experience them. What one plants and labors over will become apparent with visible evidence.

Once you've made the decision to make your mouth a ministry, you need the proper tools, nuts and bolts, and exercises to strengthen the muscles in your heart and mouth to propel your ministry (Hebrews 4:12).

Everyday life presents many opportunities for us to speak words that will produce good fruit. This book includes real-life scenarios to illuminate this point. Proverbs: 12:14 says, *"From the fruit of his lips a man is filled with good things as surely as the work of his hands rewards him."* (NIV)

It is my desire that this personal, intimate account of my life with my son will bring some level of awareness to the God-given power we have in our mouths. Making our mouths a ministry is the bridge

MAKE YOUR MOUTH A MINISTRY: *Speak Life*...

that we all must cross to discover our purpose in life and align ourselves with our destiny. Regardless of the gifts that you've been given by God, if you don't know how to control the tongue in your mouth, God will never get the glory out of anything you say or do. Your life will remain, to some extent, in darkness and you'll never experience the true essence of your destiny.

Chapter 1

Seasons of Change

I remember God speaking to me years ago about the coming of the megachurches and how they would transition to the mainstream churches to some extent. I'd never been exposed to a megachurch, so I couldn't imagine it, but I could see this movement taking place in the atmosphere. Unfortunately, I wasn't strong enough in my faith to embrace all that He was telling me about the megachurch movement and how it would change the face of the church as I know it.

In the same way, God is now speaking to me about 21st century ministry and how it will change the way I view church. Over the years I've watched ministry transition from pulpit preaching to ordinary people accepting their assignment from God as a calling to minister to others. Ephesians 4:11-13: *"And He Himself gave some to be apostles, some prophets, some evangelists, and some pastors and teachers, [12] for the equipping of the saints for the work of ministry, for the edifying of the body of Christ. [13] till we all come to the unity of the faith and of the knowledge of the Son of God, to a perfect man, to the measure of the stature of the fullness of Christ."*

This scripture helps me to justify why 21st century ministry feels like a breath of fresh air; this atmosphere allows our RELATION-

SHIP with our Heavenly Father to uplift the Kingdom of God. In addition, this fresh air in the atmosphere will allow all saints an opportunity to participate in their Father's business as they rediscover their first Love and grow intimately with Him daily. If you pursue Him, He will rekindle the romance.

Standing Boldly in the Storm

I don't know if you've ever lost someone who was so much a part of you that you struggled just to breathe in and out. If you've never experienced loss in this way, rest assured that only preparation by God can help you in the midst of this storm and the pain associated with it as you stand boldly and tell others about the goodness of Jesus. He's keeping me. The people who are in my circle of influence-- my family, my friends, strangers who I come across--anyone who knows my story, watch and constantly ask me, "How are you able to continue to stand after such loss?" My answer is simple: My relationship with the Heavenly Father.

I am close to my Heavenly Father and as a result of our relationship He knows what I need and when I need it. He wipes away my tears when I am sad. He speaks for me when I cannot speak, He carries me when I cannot even walk; in fact, He has had to breathe for me because I could not catch my breath. I might add that it has not always been like that. Somewhere along the journey I fell head over heels in love with my Heavenly Father and He prepared me for such a time as this. He now wants to prepare you through this book to stir up the latent power and exercise the "Speak Life" muscle in your mouth.

Sometimes people believe the word "loss" just means sickness then death. I have learned through this experience that loss comes in many forms. As you work through some of the exercises, you will understand better how loss can encompass necessary and unnecessary losses. for example, losses you had to embrace in order to grow up, such as lessons in love, building relationships, separation from loved ones, trust issues, unrealistic expectations, letting go, brokenness, and many more life-altering situations might be categorized as necessary losses.

However, there are other losses that might occur as a result of human intervention. For the sake of this illustration, we'll call them unnecessary losses. These losses might appear in the form of divorce, addiction, abuse, lack of self-control, even lack of self-esteem, as well as early death, violent death, suicides, and more.

This is what I know for sure: Everyone will encounter loss in one of these categories during this life's journey. We must prepare ourselves to handle the darkness or the darkness will handle us. I believe we all must strengthen the muscle in our mouths to speak life into our family, friends, co-workers, and strangers as they deal with the issues of life.

What a perfect example of what we might find in 21st century ministry: The issues of life covered in the intimacy of God and anointed for service to others.

Let me share a portion of my story.

My story falls in the unnecessary losses category. On July 1, 2005, I lost Korey, my only child. He was 33 years old. My son was a soldier. He fought mentally and emotionally to stay in a place of wellness; however, during his latter months the sickness started to consume his physical body, and darkness crept in and overshadowed the light.

During that time, I clearly remember him receiving several phone calls from co-workers, friends, family, neighbors, and others that sometimes caused him to cry. He cried because he wanted something from them that many of them were not able to give him, and that was a mouth filled with HOPE. Some of these people, not all, were within his circle of influence; that is, the people who had the greatest amount of influence on him. Although he barely had enough strength to talk, he accepted their phone calls in hopes of some life-impacting words. He didn't need anything from them but a life-building "word" that would give him some hope for tomorrow.

Unfortunately, most of the people he allowed into this deep, dark place where he resided were very uncomfortable there and didn't have a clue about what to say or how to say it. I watched him slide deeper and deeper into his dark cave and cry, phone call after phone call.

These people simply were unaware of the call upon their lives to speak words that had the power to encourage, give hope, or bring laughter--whether they whispered a prayer or sang a song. The people within his circle of influence were totally caught off guard, unprepared to answer the call. They didn't choose this call, they didn't ask for it, but one day the call showed up on their doorstep. Ready or not, this life issue put them front and center to speak life or death into someone who was so dear to them.

Most of us are no different than those in Korey's circle of influence. We haven't recognized the call upon our lives to speak to the dark places that life can take our loved ones; therefore, we're not prepared to speak life into many of the issues that our family and friends face daily. Why?

Because many of us aren't aware of the latent power in the mouths of men and women to change darkness into light--in our lives and the lives of others. As this God-given power lies dormant in the mouths of "the called," people around you are dying without hope, encouragement, laughter, prayers, songs, or love. In other words, a lifeline.

Illustration: One of the ladies in my ministry received a call at work that her son was having a seizure at school. An ambulance was transporting her son to the hospital, and school officials asked her to go there. After getting this call, she called her mother, sister, her pastor, her sisters in prayer to let them know what had happened and she needed them to pray.

Shortly the word was out that her son had a pretty bad seizure. Others in her circle of influence began to call her cell phone to ask what specifically happened and how could this happen to a child that age who had never had a seizure. They wanted to know what the doctors were saying about this and what she needed to tell the doctor and so on and so on. The mother quietly wiped her tears as she cried out to God asking Him to just save her child. Why it happened, when it happened, what caused it to happen, who saw it, and so on was not important to her at the time. These words were clouding a mind that was already in a state of being overwhelmed. In other words, these people were not prepared to speak life into the darkness that was hovering over her and her family.

Others prayed; in fact, some left their jobs and just sat in the lobby in hopes of helping with the needs of the parents. They did not ask any questions about the darkness; however, their actions and their prayers spoke life to the family, and slowly we all began to see the light at the end of the tunnel.

Exercise: Underline the darkness spoken in this illustration and highlight the movement of light spoken through the actions of those in her circle of influence.

Confronting the Darkness

I hope that you'll learn from my experiences and the experiences of others as we (the called) continue to resurrect the latent power in our mouths and exercise the "speak life" muscle. When you embrace the call to this ministry it will inspire you, stir you up, and posture you to have an encounter with God like you have never had before. My story is but one example of how necessary and unnecessary losses have unfolded in our homes, jobs, communities, and churches with no preparedness to give a lifeline.

Why are we not prepared to confront the darkness? Many of us haven't explored the possibilities of God allowing you and me (ordinary people) to witness human suffering, experience pain and loss, and step up to provide a lifeline. 21st century ministry will require you to be on the front line as this battle wages, prepared to provide a lifeline until the proper help arrives. The counselors, pastors, and teachers, are often not the front line. We as family and friends face destruction because the front line isn't ready for battle. In some cases, those in our circle of influence will never get the help they need from counselors, pastors, teachers and so on. Therefore, if we're not prepared, the people we love the most might be overtaken by the storms of life and drown.

When I talk about being "prepared," I'm not saying that you must know the Bible from cover to cover. But it's time to confront the darkness in our lives and the lives of others by preparing ourselves to be the light and salt through pursuing spiritual growth and development.

A Front-Row Seat

Most of us find ourselves in the darkness experienced by our circle of influence by virtue of relationship. We see firsthand the pain and suffering caused by being in the dark place of broken relationships, bitterness, jealousy, anger, sickness, or necessary and unnecessary losses. These consuming, negative experiences and emotions lead to frustration, discouragement, depression, and disorientation—and can cause a person to drown in the storms of life.

As family, friends, co-workers, church members, and even strangers go through various circumstances, you must be ready to speak life into them and their situations to keep the scent of death away. When someone we know is in the midst of trials and tribulations, typically we send cards, call, deliver flowers, and visit. These acts of kindness are GREAT, but seldom have we prepared our mouths to speak life (words meant to enlighten and inspire) with power and boldness; indeed, we're not purposeful in our word selection and the manifestation of the power of these words. (Sometimes just listening is the most powerful interaction, with words that can soothe pain.) In my son's case, after receiving all of the acts of kindness and hearing all the words his circle of influence had for him, he found himself in the very place he'd been fighting so hard to avoid: the place of acceptance. A man dying of thirst in the desert, for example, might give up if every place that seems to have water turns out to be a dry place. He simply accepts that there's no water.

So it was with my son. Day after day, he looked for a word of hope and encouragement; however, many times the words were soft, hollow, and without substance, turning his hopes into tears.

A Final Request

Somewhere along the journey of hope he began to accept the fact that he was dying. He started to feel hopeless and alone. I'd always been there to encourage him. He let me know that whenever he felt at his weakest, my words strengthened and encouraged him to continue to fight for wellness. He said that it was my encouraging words that helped to sustain him one day at a time as the hours turned to minutes and the minutes turned to seconds.

My son said, "Mom, you have a gift and a calling to share it." I promised him that I would write this book and let the world know that "words" (spoken or unspoken) still have power, especially when they're heartfelt. He asked me to use my ministry to teach the importance of speaking life into dark situations. This is where my son and I gave birth to Make Your Mouth a Ministry.

In April 2005, I was the keynote speaker for a women's conference at Mt. Raymond Full Gospel Baptist Church. I grew up in Mt. Raymond, located in Palmetto, Florida. That women's conference was the first place I spoke a word into a congregation about making your mouth a ministry. The response was life-changing. I give special thanks to Pastor Pollard and First Lady Versia Pollard for allowing God to use them to provide a platform for this word to go forth. Three months later I lost my son Korey.

I would like to share my 2004 Mother's Day's gift, a letter from my son.

A MOTHER'S DAY GIFT FROM A SON TO HIS MOTHER

Hi, Ma!

As I told you, I decided to do something a little different this Mother's Day. I wanted to write you a Mother's Day letter. This is not supposed to be a "Hi, how are you doing" letter. This is a letter of communications that will transfer my emotions to paper. This is a narrative letter. It's the way I feel right now, kind of like a journal entry where I make the entries but you read the notes.

Ma, this letter is to let you know how much I love you. When I think of all the things that you have been through with me, it brings tears to my eyes. Hold on, Ma, I am going to get a little intimate here. Honestly, Ma, I think sometimes how frustrating it must be for you to be my mother and, Ma, please don't think I am downing myself, but you have been there for me through so much. And I know you say, "Well, son, I am supposed to--I am your mother."

I remember when I was a little boy, I thought that I was so ugly. You would always tell me: "Don't take my word for it, just wait and see. You will find out that you are so hand-some." I couldn't hear that then, but your message never changed. I remembered you would tell me how smart I was but that did not interest me at the time. But you never stopped pushing, believing, and trying with me. Some mothers would have given up a long time ago. And WOW, Tuskegee University. The older I get the more I realize how important it was that I went to Tuskegee. Without you and Dad, I would have never finished. I didn't think I was smart enough, I didn't think I would fit in. You made me go! I was running on the push from home until one day I heard you!!!! I realized, hey, I am smart. And here's when I really realized I could do something. It's when I realized who I came from.

You know, people think that I am such a great guy, but they don't realize that I am just a fraction of what you are. You inspire me so much. You had a child at 18, the father of the child passes away, but you turned all of that into a positive. You had your baby boy. You went and got two degrees and aggressively pursued a lifestyle that would be comfortable for your son. I cannot help but love you for that. I can't help *but love you for even giving me life.*

I remember when I was a little boy in Palmetto and you would call and Grandma would go to the door and yell, "Korey, your mama is on the phone." I would run like my life depended on getting to the phone. When you would come to visit, there was no one else in the world but you and me. When I moved to Maryland, I was so happy to be with my mother, and you chose a mate that added character to your son's life. I cannot help but love you.

There are so many identical situations as ours in this world, and the outcome is much different than ours. It's amazing how you did that. You put me in some of the finest clothes and schools and made sure that I associated with the right people. You all were training me, but I didn't know that then. For that I love you and thank you.

So many things you used to tell me I see as clear as day now. It's amazing--how did you know all that stuff?

I remember at my Tuskegee graduation looking up at you all, and your faces were so bright and happy. That made me happy, that's why I gave you the degree. At that time I was doing it for you but I don't think you cared if I was doing it for you. You just wanted me to do it.

Sometimes I wonder why am I so blessed to have the best mother in the world. You are the most positive person I know, and I need that in my life. I also want to thank you for encouraging my relationship with Jesus Christ. Because of you, Grandma, and Dad, I know where to go when things of this world get too tough!! I love you so much, Ma. Please tell me if you like my Mother's Day letter.

P.S. You know there is much more.

Chapter 2

Speaking Life as a Spiritual Calling

After losing my son and looking back over the footprints of my life, I'm convinced that there's a divine call upon every human being to speak life into their surroundings. It seems as though we're all connected through our life experiences.

I also believe that the family that you were born into has everything to do with your preparation for your purpose and destiny, which is developed through your relationship with God and the people He has put in your path. As we navigate through our various relationships, our mouths play a major role in reaching our God-given destiny. If we can agree that the mouth plays a major role, then we can agree that we can't allow our mouths to run freely, unchecked and out of control. We must take control of this mouth and train it, seek the tools to control it, manage it and keep it in check, realizing that our purpose and destiny are in the balance.

Just imagine embracing the concept of speaking life as a "spiritual calling." Accepting this call wholeheartedly and being a witness to the changes in our families lives, workplaces, relationships, community interactions, outreach in our churches, and in the human race -- one word at a time -- will allow us to see how great our God is.

WOW!

This is possible by embracing the call and preparing yourself for battle. I hope that you understand at this point that I believe that most of us aren't equipped to overcome our emotions and say the life-building words needed at the right time without the necessary tools. The tool kit is the "Speak Life" muscle-building section of the book. This section presents six principles and assessments that will equip you to transcend the darkness in your life and the lives around you.

If we, as ordinary people, would accept the call to "speak life" in our circle of influence, many of our family and friends would live (lively) and not die (lifeless) in dark situations. When we get a glimpse of how to use the transforming power in our mouths to get this darkness off of our backs, we'll begin to see everyday folks become extraordinary people through the power of the Holy Spirit. We'll see the power of the breath of life as it does the work of turning around drug addicts, prostitutes, alcoholics, liars and so on.

A Clear Definition

When I speak at conferences, churches, companies, and/or schools and give examples of how to speak to the darkness in someone's life, inevitably someone will corner me off and tell me how they're presently living that situation.

Sometimes we don't make the connection between our spiritual calling to speak life and its effect on the world around us. Let's look a little deeper at what "speak life as a spiritual calling" means in this book.

We need to define four key words to ensure that we're all on the same page.

Key Word - SPIRITUAL

The first is "spiritual." The Merriam Webster Dictionary says the word "spiritual" means "related or joined in spirit"

Key Word - CALLING

A strong inner impulse toward a particular course of action, especially when accompanied by conviction of divine influence.

Key Word - LIFE

The third word, "life," means a way or manner of living.

The fourth and final word is

Key Word - SPEAKING

"Speaking," which means to utter words or articulate sounds with the ordinary voice : TALK b (1) : to express thoughts, opinions, or feelings orally.

For the sake of this book, when we say "speaking life as a spiritual calling," we mean that you've invited a higher power (the Holy Spirit) in your life and He will give you the words to speak to the darkness that comes in your life or someone else's. Your life experience has created a unique path that will call you to speak to certain situations in a heartfelt way. This is important because growing spiritually is driven by your experiences, not just your knowledge. Something you experienced during a previous season of your life may prepare and position you to be the only one in your circle of influence who can speak to that situation. The idea of someone's mouth being a tool for ministry is so far-fetched for some people that they won't be able to wrap their minds around this spiritual calling.

In the March 2005 issue of *Beauty for Ashes* – more than a magazine, I wrote about my call to ministry as a spiritual calling. I couldn't wrap my mind around this principle at the time either but I decided to "walk in obedience!"

2005 Beauty for Ashes Article - Walking in Obedience

Deborah Leaner Ministries is excited about celebrating the second anniversary of walking in obedience to God's will. We've been blessed to witness the lives of women being restored, equipped, and transformed in extraordinary ways. Many of them have come back to disciple other women through the word of God. They've aligned themselves with their destiny and purpose through this ministry. Thank you, Lord!

I could not have imagined what God would do simply because I was obedient to the vision He had given me.

The seed for DLM was planted in 1997 after completing a one-year intense discipleship-training course that completely changed my life. In April 2002 I began to walk in what the Lord had inspired me to do, which was disciple other women.

In January 2003, I stepped out on faith, creating Divine Dis-

cipleship for Sisters. This discipleship course began with five spirit-filled, eager women. They graduated in August 2003 equipped, restored, and transformed.

The second DDS class began in September 2003 with 17 women and five co-laborers. These extraordinary women graduated physically and spiritually April 17, 2004. They presented and hosted DLM's first Unique Women's Conference. It was AWESOME!

I am so excited to present to you our third generation of DLM women. Each one has been handpicked by God to take this journey with Him. He is calling each of us to a more intimate relationship with Him that will restore, equip, and transform us to walk in our destiny. We are humbled to be God's instruments as we disciple 55 women. Sixteen extraordinary women disciplined in the word of God will walk in obedience with these ladies weekly as co-laborers. WOW! We give thanks and praise to our God for His goodness and kindness extended toward this ministry.

In December 2003 the ministry broadened its mission with the publication of Beauty for Ashes, a magazine written by and for Christian women.

It seems like yesterday when we sat around Keeley Lucas' dining room table in Washington, DC, talking about the vision God had given me about the Beauty for Ashes publication. Now we are celebrating the one-year anniversary. Again I have to shout WOW!

As we obey God's will, our lives change. Sister Keeley became the editor for Beauty for Ashes and brought us from a mighty long way. She has passed the baton to our next Editor in Chief, Sister Jean Marrow, who walks in obedience to the God-given vision for this publication. Eight gifted, talented women also are walking in obedience with Sister Jean. God equipped each of them to take Beauty for Ashes to the next level. Expect growth and pray for continued obedience to God's vision for this publication.

It has indeed been a blessing to be chosen by God to work

with these women. I thank Him daily for using my life as a vehicle to manifest His will.

Out of Loss, Ministry

This article is just another illustration of that unique path that I spoke about earlier. As human spirits, we have an innate calling on our lives that draws us to places of destiny and purpose just as we gravitate to dance, music, writing, or math. God gave all of us a mouth or a way to communicate His desires. If we allow Him to govern what comes out of our mouths, we'll understand that this is a universal calling by virtue of relationships.

It works like this: Through His grace, God can use our failures in life. He allows us to help someone else out of his/her darkness with the very things that caused us to fall. In order for God's grace to kick in, however, I believe you must have a repentant heart. You've seen it before--a person's issue of life becomes public, and we can tell if God is dealing with his or her heart based on what comes out of the person's mouth. The Bible says in Proverbs 4:23, "keep your heart with all diligence, for out of it spring the issues of life." In some cases the person becomes a true advocate for that issue of life.

In my personal experiences with family and friends who have experienced intense pain after necessary or unnecessary loss, one of two things will happen:

1. You sense a higher calling in the earth realm upon your life.

2. You become bitter and shut down as a result of the darkness.

I want to bring some light or awareness to your circumstances. When pain occurs in your life, I believe that you must connect your deep, heartfelt thirst for answers and for understanding to a higher power. Submitting to a higher power will often start the healing process needed to mend a broken heart, thereby assuring proper alignment with the mouth. This alignment will create an atmosphere around you that will breathe life, not death, in you and your circle of influence.

On the other hand, if your inward look causes you to become bitter, you will sour the atmosphere around you. This toxic waste will spill out of your mouth, and the scent will be unbearable.

I will continue to use my story to encourage you to prepare for the call. Through the darkness and suffering I experienced, God has drawn me closer to Him and prepared me for ministry. I was called to this and I now have a burden to tell others about the light that brightened my darkness. As I explained earlier, everyone will have some darkness in this life; therefore, it's my prayer that everyone who reads this book will allow it to prepare and equip them to speak life into their family, friends, and strangers' lives.

I'm humbled that God would use my story to help others put the pieces back together and learn to live after loss. If we want to make our mouths a ministry, we must tell others of the goodness of Jesus and how He brought light to our darkness. In others words, tell your story. No one can tell your story better than you.

God creates daily opportunities for us to make our mouths a minis- try, so we must accept the charge and equip ourselves to speak life and throw out a lifeline to anyone living in darkness. Real-life issues go on around us daily, and we don't have to look very far to find them. If you look carefully at the lives of the people closest to you, you'll find broken relationships, depression, thoughts of suicide, the repercussions of rape and molestation, sickness, death, and more. By virtue of reading this book, I believe that God has called you to understand your purpose and destiny as it relates to your mouth. No matter where you are or how you serve in the body of Christ, you must first learn to speak life (liveliness) and not death (doom) in the lives of others. Join me as I continue to stir up the latent power that lies dormant in my mouth. Stir up the God-given power to speak life and not death in your circle of influence.

Chapter 3

Your Mouth Ain't No River, But It Sure Will Drown You

My mother had six sisters and three brothers, and most of them lived within five miles of each other. They'd see each other and talk on a daily basis. On Friday nights they'd go out on the town and leave the children with Grandma.

When all of the children would get together at Grandma's house, I always wanted to share something with the other grandchildren. I was very talkative, never at a loss for words. The thing that I remember most about those Friday nights is my grandmother telling me, "Deborah, your mouth ain't no river, but it will surely drown you."

Sad to say, this parable is alive and well in the 21st century. "Your mouth ain't no river, but it will surely drown you" played itself out in my life and in the lives of others over and over again. I'm amazed that something my grandmother told me 40 years ago is still actively destroying lives today.

This is why we're still writing about the power in the mouths of mankind.

Have you ever said something to someone or about someone and it caused a level of destruction that you didn't intend? If you have, then you have joined the ranks of many of us who have lived and learned that "your mouth ain't no river but it will surely drown you."

It was really hard for me to learn that my intentions weren't justification enough to detour the pain and damage that I've caused in my life and in the lives of others with the nasty words that have come out of my mouth. I remember the days when someone would say something to me that didn't set well with me. My flesh would rise, and I had no problem giving them a piece of my mind. When I reflect on those times I know that I caused some level of pain to myself and to the other person.

That was then and this is now. Now when the flesh rises, it's a trigger for me to examine my heart by asking for help from my Father above. Here's how:

- I talk to God about how someone is speaking to me as they are speaking and they don't have a clue as to why they're not getting a rise out of me.

- When the person finishes, God speaks through my mouth, because my heart is so deep into His heart that you can't separate the two of us.

I can't do this alone. I need God to guard my heart. The scripture says *"Above all else, guard your heart, for everything you do flows from it"* (Proverbs 4:23, TNIV). This tells me that I must guard my heart 24/7, monitor it, and maintain it because it is easy to become defiled by lapsing back to those old thoughts and habits. This also lets me know that you can't easily separate the heart and the mouth; indeed, they are two different parts of the body but they're inseparable. As mentioned in the above scripture, if we don't guard our hearts 24/7 some wicked stuff will pour out of our mouths.

Generally when you see or hear prideful statements, covetous desires, bitterness, jealousy, and abusive adjectives, it is a sign that our hearts are unprotected from participating on some level in an environment that breeds this wickedness. Malicious words will show up when we least expect them if we continue to reside in this type of atmosphere. An unguarded heart will cause spiritual defilement, according to Mark 7:14-23.

A Lifeline from Solomon

In the book of Proverbs, Solomon gives some much-needed wisdom for those who are drowning in the rivers of their mouths. His guidance will give you a lifeline to apply daily to your life. You can pass this lifeline on to friends, family members, and others as you begin speaking into their lives.

Prov. 4:23-26 NKJ

- In chapter 4:1, Solomon tells us to *"Hear, my children, the instruction of a father, and give attention to know understanding."* In other words, pay attention to what Solomon is saying so that you can truly understand how to live this life.

- In verse 4:23, He says, *"Keep your heart with all diligence for out of it spring the issues of life."*

- 4:24, He tells us to *"Put away from you a deceitful mouth and put perverse lips far from you."*

- 4:25, He tells us to *"Let your eyes look straight ahead and your eyelids look right before you."*

- 4:26, he tells us *"Ponder the path of your feet, and let all your ways be established."*

I thought it best to present some stories that will illustrate how the wisdom that Solomon gave in Proverbs 4:1, 23, 24, 25, and 26 could have helped my mouth and the mouths of others who caused great pain and displeasure. You also will have the opportunity in this chapter to participate by writing a few stories that changed the course of your life by the words spoken to you. Then apply Solomon's wisdom to those stories and see if you can transcend some of the hurt and pain you encountered by empowering yourself to create a new ending based on the new principles.

As you participate in this exercise you'll find that we're continually in need of much of Solomon's wisdom. We also need others around us who can hold us accountable for speaking life-impacting words on a daily basis into ourselves and our circle of influence.
However, it will take practice, practice, and more practice.

Story No. 1
The Cheerleader's Mom

It was a Friday night and our football team was playing one of the local football rivals in a home game. The atmosphere was exciting, the band was practicing, and the majorettes and drill teams were all dressed for the occasion. The football teams were under the bright lights on the football field throwing passes. It seemed like every teenager in town was at the game to see who would win.

For me it was the most important game of the world because I had just become a cheerleader alternate. If one of the girls were out for any reason, I would get to cheer. Well, I received the call that I needed to get to the game a little earlier because one of the cheerleaders was sick and they were making arrangements to pick up her uniform so that I could wear it that night until my uniform came in, which was common practice.

I was so excited I couldn't remember my words to the cheer. I called everyone I knew to let them know that I'd be cheering that night because for me and my school this would be the first time an African American cheerleader performed in the history of the school.

When my parents dropped me off in front of the gym, I saw everyone outside in pre-game mode, but not the cheerleaders. In my excitement I ran looking everywhere for them and I couldn't find them, so I thought I would check the locker room for any last-minute announcements.

When I walked into the locker room the atmosphere was gloom and doom. "What's the problem?" I asked. Shortly after asking that question, I learned that I was the problem. The head cheerleader came over and said that when the cheerleader who was sick told her mom who was going to be wearing her uniform, that mother said something to the effect of a "nigger" would not ever wear her daughter's uniform. They didn't have another uniform for me to wear. So I was unable to cheer that night, and the air was filled with strife, disappointment, and anger.

In Proverbs 4:23, Solomon tells us to keep our hearts with all diligence. The cheerleader's mom illustrates the pain and hurt that just a few words can cause to the lives of others when we don't guard our heart. However, it was equally important that I and my circle of influence guard our hearts so that our mouths would not spew out the same prejudice as this cheerleader mom.

Obviously, some degree of prejudice was in this mother's heart towards African Americans; after all, I certainly had done nothing to this lady. When she encountered this "issue of life," her heart spoke for her mouth and destroyed everything within sight, including her own daughter's future ability to build relationships without prejudice. This mother's words changed the atmosphere of the cheerleading squad from that day forward.

Write about a time during your childhood when someone spoke words so devastating, they shaped a part of your life. Apply Solomon's wisdom and write a different ending to the story.

Story No. 2
Workplace Drama

A senior vice president of an organization directed a vice president to make some decisions that conflicted with her moral standards. As a female, she felt powerless, as if she had no one to hear and understand her concerns. Other women worked in the office, of course, but she was reluctant to share her thoughts because she wasn't sure she could trust them with the information.

Another woman in the organization worked as a senior-level manager in a different department. The vice president had some level of relationship with this woman and felt that she would be safe in sharing her heart. She did and that decision caused the vice president to lose (loss) her entire career in that field. The very next morning she was called into the big office, where she was greeted by the senior vice president. She was reprimanded and suspended for being disloyal. The manager had gone to the higher-ups, saddened by her treachery.

The vice president had risen through the ranks and gained her position through hard work and diligence. She was devastated when she returned to work after her suspension only to find that the officers of that organization decided to terminate her. This situation caused the company and the families involved a tremendous amount of time and money, all because of a lack of understanding about the power of the words in the vice president's mouth.

Write about how devastating words spoken in the workplace shaped a part of your life. Apply Solomon's wisdom and write a different ending to the story.

Story No. 3
The Untold Story

Five women were working on a project in a newsroom that would change their personal and professional relationships forever. The team was analyzing the details of the project to determine what would be appropriate for public distribution.

One of the ladies shared the sensitive nature of one story and suggested that the group members should walk softly as they interacted with the writer of the story because of the story's confidential nature. The entire team discussed the pros and cons of keeping the writer's name confidential due to the subject matter. As the team got closer to the public deadline, one of the team members needed to speak with this writer. After speaking with the writer, the writer immediately called the team member that she told the story to and questioned her integrity based on the lack of respect and sensitivity for such confidential information shown by a member of her staff. The writer of the story exploded, demanded to remove her story from the publication, and requested an apology and some time to cool off before meeting to resolve this issue.

Needless to say, the final publication didn't include this story, and disloyalties and distrust on all levels caused damage and destruction to the work at hand. Further, others who could have been blessed by the information never saw it.

Write about a time when someone shared confidential information and created a misunderstanding so devastating that it shaped a part of your life. Apply Solomon's wisdom and write a different ending to the story.

Story No. 4
Does it Really Take a Village to Raise a Child?

One of the teachers in the teachers' lounge shared a story about an experience she had as a teacher's assistant. She said: I witnessed a teacher sharing with a parent how her child inappropriately behaves in her class. The teacher suggested to the parent that she should mention to her child that this behavior is in appropriate and suggested ways to address this behavior in the future. The teacher who offered the advice was confronted by the mother, who was offended by the suggestions. The mother informed the teacher that she had a circle of family and friends, whom she relied upon to give her suggestions on how to raise her child and felt strongly that she did not want any out side influence.

The teacher's assistant said this is the type of question that is always in the minds of teachers. Certainly the teacher could do more, but parents are raising their children based on different values than in generations past. The truth is that parents make the decisions about how they want their children raised and sometimes they must be flexible and accept that we have to expand the village in order to raise our children.

Write about something you said to or about a child to her mom/dad that caused such pain and devastation, those words shaped a part of your life. Apply Solomon's wisdom and write a different ending to the story.

As we resurrect the voices of those who spoke pain into our paths, the words of wisdom that Solomon offers can heal some of the hurt and create a new ending. Just as this wisdom can impart a new ending for our darkness, we can share this experience anew in our lives and offer this advice to our circle of influence. Further, we can pass on wisdom to current and future generations.

I Didn't Mean To Hurt Your Feelings!

Just because you didn't intend to cause pain doesn't justify the damage that you might have caused with your words. When you take responsibility and realize that you don't have to say everything you're thinking, you become selective and in control of what comes out of your mouth.

Just for illustrative purposes, think of your words as a bowling ball. Imagine you're holding a bowling ball (your words) and then releasing it down the alley. The ball spins and knocks down every pin in its way.

Now imagine those pins as your family and friends. How many of those people have been knocked down by the words that you've said? What about other family and friends who weren't prepared to speak life when trouble threatened someone's life?

Negativity forms itself much like a bowling ball (it's generally big, dark, and ready to roll). As it barrels into our lives, it destroys everything in its path. It rips through families by way of strife and bitterness, and it wounds the downtrodden by way of insensitivity

and carelessness. When our words are cold, hard, and lifeless, they destroy the lives of those who care about us.

When words come to mind and you're dying to tell somebody, whether it's gossip with a co-worker or an angry outburst to the lady in the grocery store who cuts you off with her cart, try this filtering exercise. Ask yourself these four questions. If you can't answer all of them appropriately, then STOP and do one of two things: Don't say anything at all or find a new way to get your point across.

Filtering Exercise

Are you angry? You should never say or do anything out of anger. In Ephesians 4:26, Paul said to *"Be angry, and do not sin."* He must have known that anger causes us to say or do things we'll regret later. Remember that we mustn't "give place to the devil," for he comes to kill, steal, and destroy. What better way for him to do this than by using you? If you are angry just keep your mouth closed.

Have you prayed? Jesus says in Matthew 26:41 that we are to *"Watch and pray, lest you enter not into temptation. The spirit indeed is willing, but the flesh is weak."* We're born with an overwhelming desire to please the flesh because we're born in sin. Through prayer we align ourselves with the spirit of God. Ask God for help in your heart before you utter a word.

Is this something that Jesus would say? If what you're about to say isn't said in love, then it doesn't represent what Jesus would say. *"He who does not love does not know God, for God is love."* (I John 4:8).

Is there any chance that someone could perceive your words in a negative way? *Proverbs 4:14-15 tells us "Do not enter the path of the wicked, and do not walk in the way of evil."*

Chapter 4

The ABC's of Developing a Ministry in Your Mouth

101 Ways to Make Your Mouth A Ministry
A quick reference for speaking life

1. Learn from your mistakes.

2. Ask God for forgiveness and forgive yourself.

3. Talk to friends who love you and your mistakes (we need girlfriends).

4. Identify who's talking too much in your Circle of Influence and pray for that person.

5. Thank God for divine connections.

6. Meditate on what you'll say before saying it.

7. Chew on what you're told before throwing up on others.

8. Ask God when to speak.

9. Who does the man in your life say you are?

10. Who are you in love with now?

11. Apologize.

12. Laugh when you don't want to.

13. Sing a new song.

14. Pray a prayer of surrender to God.

15. Load your lips with righteousness.

16. Know what you're trying to say.

17. Be reflective - get a good understanding of what others are

saying to you.

18.   Bring a word from the Lord.

19.   Wait on the Lord.

20.   Keep your mouth closed.

21.   Stay divinely connected.

22.   Write it up first.

23.   Know when to wrap it up.

24.   Hear through the ears of Christ.

25.   Paint your words.

26.   Become a supplier of living words.

27.   Speak with passion and pleasure.

28.   Be a woman of your word.

29.   Speak words that enlighten.

30.   Clothe yourself in the garment of gratitude.

31.   Say you will do it (affirm yourself).

32.   Strive to speak correctly.

33.   Be a great speaker of words that change lives.

34.   Work on developing a global mouth (read).

35.   Present more than words when you speak.

36.   Do your words represent who you are?

37.   Learn the power of your words.

38.   Use words to light up the room.

39.   Be a good listener.

40.   Know when to zip (mouth) it up.

41.   Pick up your emotions with your words.

42.   Speak it into existence.

43.   Build a strong vocabulary.

44.   Master your mouth-- don't be a know-it-all.

45.   Speak with joy.

46.   Know when to talk and when to hold your thoughts.

47.   What is your body language saying?

48.   Strive to bring life into the lives of others through your words.

49.   Speak with confidence.

50.   Be known as a woman who makes beautiful words.

51.   Make your mouth a ministry.

52.   Routinely wash out your mouth.

53.   Spread the Word (Gospel).

54.   Sweet dreams (plant good thoughts).

55.   Learn the "Art of Apology."

56.   Don't talk to hear yourself talk.

57.   Express yourself with dignity.

58. What words are you digesting?

59. Smile!

60. Get a handle on your words.

61. Be thankful that you can speak.

62. Be a woman of few words.

63. Work for the word (ministry).

64. Guard your mouth.

65. Say "Thank You."

66. Speak clearly now.

67. Use words with wisdom.

68. Chase after the word of God.

69. Speak the Truth boldly.

70. Look for opportunities to be quiet; someone will ask you to speak.

71. Rest your lips.

72. A mouth filled with garbage stinks.

73. What are spiritual lips?

74. People can feel words from the heart.

75. Speak to your neighbors -- create a positive atmosphere in your neighborhood.

76. The word of your testimony will speak for you.

77. Take an assessment of your words and determine if your life follows your words.

78. Elevate your words--take the high road.

79. Watch your mouth and where it is taking you.

80. Invest in your mouth (practice the right words).

81. Speaking your mind isn't the answer.

82. Acquire an exquisite taste for the word of God.

83. Articulate your words with assurance.

84. Identify where those ugly words come from.

85. Be responsible for (own) your words.

86. Recognize hurtful words.

87. Respond to gossip with a deaf ear.

88. Redeem the Word of God.

89. Slanderous words - drop them from your vocabulary.

90. Use words that resurrect liveliness.

91. There is no reward for lies.

92. Pay close attention to the fragrance of your words.

93. Control the "Power Tool" in your mouth - the tongue.

94. Tune your tone - check the rhythm in your voice when talking to someone.

95. Opening words set the tone.

96.   Lose the prideful tongue.

97.   Freshen your breath.

98.   Pray for your mouth.

99.   Season your words.

100.   Use peaceful words.

101.   Check your heartbeat for God.

The ABC's of Developing a Ministry in Your Mouth

The relationship between the mouth and the heart must come under the submission of the Holy Spirit in order for you to make your mouth a ministry. In Matthew 15:8, Jesus says, *"These people draw near to me with their mouth and honor me with their lips, but their heart is far from me."* In this passage Jesus reveals the conflict between the hearts and the mouths of the scribes and the Pharisees. This is a perfect example of how the conflict shows up in our own lives. People can generally tell when you're giving lip service to their problems and issues as opposed to having gone through the same circumstance yourself or having a passion for that particular life challenge.

When you align your heart and mouth with the truth (word of God), you'll give birth to your ministry. When this happens, your ministry will supply a double portion of anointing and set you up to be a blessing to others. My experience has been that once you use the fruit of your lips for uplifting the Kingdom, blessing will overtake you. Season the words that come out of your mouth with the truth so that God will allow you to see in your life the promise He made to Abraham in Hebrews 6:14.

Making your mouth a ministry also allows you to speak with your destiny in mind. The mouth speaks blessings and curses. If you speak truth to others, they'll be blessed and so will you. On the other hand, if you speak curses (darkness) into others, they'll die (spiritually) and so will you.

When you're clear about the alignment of the mouth and the heart and others begin to benefit from your talk and walk in the word, you're ready to walk into your ministry. You'll have learned to successfully serve others and die to yourself.

Listed below are the ABC's outlined in this book to help you walk into your destiny with boldness.

A = **Abide** - *Abide so that you can bear fruit. John 15:5*

B = **Be yourself** - *God created you. Nobody can be you better than you. Genesis 1:31*

C = **Confess** - *He is faithful to forgive our sins. 1 John 1:9*

D = **Dream** - *Joseph had a dream. Gen. 37:5*

E = **Established** – *Root yourself in the word of God. Col. 2:7*

F = **Forgive** - *Learn to forgive yourself and you'll find forgiving others might be easier. Matt. 6:12, 14*

G = **Grace** – *We need it. 2 Corinthians 8:9*

H = **Heart** – *Allow the peace of God to guard your heart. Phil. 4:7*

I = **Idle** - *An enemy 1 Timothy 5:13*

J = **Jesus** – *Get to know him personally Luke 9:23*

K = **Knowledge** - *The word is knowledge Exodus 35:31*

L = **Love** - *Always remember that God really LOVES you! John 15:12*

M = **Make Your Mouth a Ministry**- *Get off the pew and get involved in the Great Commission. Matt. 28:19*

N = **Need** - *If you are in need of anything know that He will supply all of your needs. Phil 4:19*

O = **Obedience** – *Have confidence in obedience. Philemon 1:21*

P = **People Building** - *You must build relationships Philp.2:4*

Q=Quiet Spirit - *The beauty of a gentle and quiet spirit*

    1 Peter 3:4

R=Reconciliation - *We have the gift of reconciliation- "All this is*

    from God, who through Christ reconciled us to himself and

    gave us the Ministry of reconciliation." 2 Corinthians 5:18

S = Slaying Your Giants *2 Samuel 21:14-16*

T=Think - *For I know the thoughts that I think toward you, says*

    the LORD, thoughts of peace and not of evil, to give

    you a future and a hope. Jeremiah 29:11

U = Unity - *Unity and diversity in one Body - "For as the body is*

    one and has many members, but all the members of that one

    body, being many, are one body, so also is Christ."

    1 Corinthians 12:12

V = Vision - *The vision is yet for an appointed time. Habakkuk 2:3*

W=Wisdom - *God gives wisdom. 1 Chronicles 22:12*

X = X-ray - *Examine your heart- Psalm 26:2*

Y = Yoke - *"For my yoke is easy and my burden is light."*

    Matt 11:30

Z = Zion - *The city of David. Psalm 50:2*

PART II

Making Your Mouth A Ministry in Everyday Life

Chapter 5

Visit To Refreshing Waters

It was a typical day at Refreshing Waters. Busy! Customers flowed in and out of the spa all day long. The phones were ringing off the hook with appointments, and other customers in the lounge waited to receive their treatments. Inside of the spa, I noticed two ladies sitting next to each other having a conversation. They introduced themselves as Katie and Rebecca. They didn't appear to know each other; however, that didn't stop them from chatting.

When it was time for their spa services, their technicians, Carla and Susan, called them both at the same time to receive pedicures. Co-incidentally, both technicians worked beside each other.

Carla had recently changed spa locations to work at Refreshing Wa-ters. The way things looked, a lot of her clients followed her there because she was booked solid today. All of Carla's clients knew she loved doing what she does best: ensuring the comfort of her clients and serving them with excellence. As Carla was giving Katie, her long-time client, a pedicure, Katie said to her, "I won't be coming out here on a regular basis for my manicure and pedicure now that you're way out here in no man's land. Your new location is entirely too far away from my house and it will be a major inconvenience for me to travel this far out for my spa treatment."

Carla said, "I'm sorry to hear that. If it's too far for you to travel and you like my old location better, ask for my mother-in law when you're ready to make your next appointment. She does great work! I'm sure she would be happy to service you."

While they were conversing, Susan and Rebecca sat quietly beside them listening in on their conversation as Susan gave Rebecca a pedicure.

Katie said, "Please, I don't like your mother-in law. I would go any-where else before I allowed her to touch me. Remember the time your mother-in-law said that you couldn't do nails? Or how about the times she cheated her clients out of their money? Now she has to be watched at all times because she can't be trusted."

"You can't be talking about my mother-in-law," Carla said. "My mother-in-law has blonde hair and wears a pink apron." "That is exactly who I am talking about! She told me how nasty you were. Don't you remember?"

After hearing all of the mean things Katie was saying about her mother-in-law, Carla excused herself for a few minutes and went to the ladies' room.

When Carla returned from the ladies' room, Susan said in a consoling voice, "Did your mother-in-law really say those things about you? That's terrible! If I were you, I would tell my husband she's not welcome in our house and I'd have nothing to do with her if she's going to continue to bad mouth you to other clients. Rebecca, what do you think?"

"You're supposed to be a woman of God. I really don't know the whole story. Now, when are you going to start on my nails?"

After hearing Susan and Rebecca's responses, Katie said in a loud voice, "I don't care who agrees or disagrees with me. I will spend my money where I want to spend it."

Carla's spirit clearly was broken after hearing such mean things about her mother-in-law and the comments her mother-in-law had supposedly said. Carla knew some of it was true, but she didn't want reminders because she'd forgiven her mother-in-law. Hearing it again was like having a scab ripped off a sore, re-injuring the wound. The whole time Katie was there, Carla's spirit remained low. Her eyes stayed red and swollen from fighting back the tears. As a result of the turmoil caused by Katie's conversation, Carla looked like she'd been punched in the face.

Here we are at the spa, a place designed to give people somewhere to go to escape their stressful environments for a moment of relaxation and enjoyment in a peaceful, calm atmosphere. This day, however, the spa's atmosphere was far from its original purpose. Katie had created the opposite with her words.

To understand why Katie's heart is in the shape it's in, we'll need to trace the surface pain coming out of her mouth to the root cause of the pain in her heart.

Use the story as a backdrop to answer the questions. Allow the Holy Spirit to teach you as you answer these questions. If you do this exercise with the Holy Spirit, He will work on your heart. Remember Matthew 12:34b, "For out of the abundance of the heart the mouth speaks."

1. How would you characterize the condition of Katie's heart?

2. What factors would you attribute to Katie's heart condition?

3. How would you reconcile Katie's "heart" condition to her words?

4. How did the other women at the spa help or hinder the situation?

5. If Katie were in your "circle of influence," how could you help in her healing process?

Moments of Reflection:

1. I want you to think back to a time when you had a conversation or gave advice to someone who was hurting from someone else's wrongdoing. Remember how much they were afflicted? What was your response? Could you have handled it better?

2. What will you do to ensure that your words are pleasant and bring life to the situation, not death?

Pray and meditate on these scriptures:

James 1:19 – Wherefore, my beloved brethren, let me, (insert your name), be swift to hear, slow to speak, slow to wrath.

I Thessalonians 5:11 – Therefore, I (insert your name), will encourage others and build each one up.

II Thessalonians 2:16,17 – May our Lord Jesus Christ himself and God our Father, who loved me, (insert your name), and by his grace gave me, (insert your name), eternal encouragement and good hope, encourage my heart and strengthen me in every good deed and word.

Chapter 6

Meeting in the Ladies' Room

Almost everyone watched Monique when she came into work on Friday because she'd never been late for work. Her co-workers knew immediately that something had happened. Her eyes were red and swollen. Her beautiful smile had turned into a frown. She had on the same clothes she wore yesterday. She was a mess.

Monique sat in her cubicle without saying anything to anyone. The phones didn't ring and no one else in the office said a word. The office was so quiet you could hear a pin drop. After sitting there for five minutes or so, she said to Lea and Liberty, sitting in cubicles across from her, "MEET ME IN THE LADIES' ROOM." Everyone watched as the women walked out of the office together.

As soon as she entered the ladies' room, Monique started to cry uncontrollably. Lea and Liberty became very concerned. Why was she so overwhelmed with grief and tears? All they could do was put their arms around her to console her the best way they could at that moment.

When she finally got herself together, Monique said, "My babysitter, Candy, called me last night and told me that she has been having an affair with my husband, Jim, for over two years. She said that she could prove it because she could describe different body marks on Jim's private parts. She said that she had given Jim an ultimatum. The ultimatum was upon his return from Dallas today, he would leave me. In other words, ask for a divorce or the relationship with her would be over. Then, before she hung up with me, she said, "By the way, Monique, I am pregnant."

Monique had been looking forward to going to the airport with her kids to meet Jim when his plane arrived. After this news, however, her emotions were so out of control that going to the airport was the last thing on her mind. All she could think about was strangling Jim. In the midst of her tears, Monique confided that she felt devastated, humiliated, betrayed, embarrassed, and destroyed.

Lea interrupted and said in an angry, revengeful voice, "What you need to do is go over to Candy's house and strangle her to death for messing with your man. You can't go out like this. In fact, I will go and KICK her behind for you. How dare she call you and drop a bomb like that over the phone! GIRRRLL, you need to beat her to death."

Lea went on to say, "This must be the most devastating experience that anyone can go through. The mental, physical, and emotional pain is more than anyone could bear. I would beat her to death and probably kill myself afterward because this is just too much to bear. The shock from news like this can give you a heart attack and para-lyze you emotionally. Girl, you've been injured for life."

Liberty commanded Lea to be quiet. "This is not about you," she said firmly. "This is about Monique, her husband, and family." Turn-ing to Monique, Liberty said, "First of all, I would like to take you home now, if you agree, because I don't think work is the best place for you right now. When you get home, we'll come up with a plan and figure out the best way to get your husband from the airport. I'll also pick the kids up from school and my son, Cory, can take all the kids to the movies. Because it's the weekend, I'll arrange for a sleepover at my house so that the kids can stay with my family this weekend."

Her voice softened as she continued to speak to Monique. "I know your mind is spinning and flooded with intense emotions; however, you have to manage your feelings enough to speak to the kids and give them your blessing for a weekend sleepover. Tell them that a friend of Jim's will bring him home so they won't worry. In addition, I know a very good crisis counselor at my church who has worked with this type of situation before, so if you don't mind I'd like to call him and get some professional advice." Monique agreed, and Liberty left the restroom to call the counselor.

Join the Conversation in the Ladies' Room

I would like to give you the opportunity to give Monique some advice based on her situation. It's your turn to speak to Monique.

What would you say to Monique?

Based on the conversation you had with Monique in the above exercise, reflect upon your advice to Monique and assess the impact your words had in her life.

1. The words you spoke to Monique, where did they come from?

2. Did they come from a healthy experience or a bad experience? Explain the experience.

3. How did these words make you feel as you spoke them?

4. Did you feel good, like you were in charge or perhaps empowered? Why?

5. Did you feel you were helpful? Why? Were there feelings of sorrow or embarrassment?

6. Were your words vengeful?

7. Who or what influenced your words (your truth)?

8. What "legs" (experiences) built your belief?

9. When did you embrace those spoken words as your truth?

Moments of Reflection:

1. I want you to think back to a time when you had a conversation or gave advice to someone who was hurting from someone else's hurtful words. Remember how much they were afflicted? What was your response? Could you have handled it better?

2. What will you do to ensure that your words are pleasant and bring life to the situation, not death?

Pray and meditate on these scriptures:

Psalm 19:14, Let the words of my mouth, and the meditation of my heart, be acceptable in thy sight, O LORD, my strength, and my redeemer.

Philippians 4:7, and the peace of God, which passeth all understanding, shall guard (insert your name) heart and (insert your name) thoughts in Christ Jesus.

Psalms 34:13 – I, (insert your name), will keep my tongue from evil, and lips from speaking guile or deceit.

Chapter 7

Your Tone is
Out of Tune

It's Monday morning, and Shelly is preparing herself mentally for a busy workweek. As she leaves the house, she notices how beautiful the weather is outside. The sun is shining, the birds are singing, and a fresh breeze is blowing in the air. Before Shelly gets into the car, she inhales deeply and then whispers a short prayer: "Thank you, God, for a beautiful morning." It was what she needed to put herself in the right frame of mind to expect a good day.

While driving to work she couldn't help but think about her client's case that she had been working long and hard on for a week and the work that was still left to complete. In addition to this client's case, she thought about the women's ministry meeting that she had to attend that night. She had a lot on her plate; however, the weather put her in such a good mood, she was ready to tackle whatever she had to do.

When Shelly got to her office she made herself a cup of coffee and immediately went to work. Later on that day, around lunchtime, Shelly's supervisor, Barbara, called her on the phone to let her know that she had another case for Shelly. Barbara also wanted Shelly to meet the client that night. Shelly was familiar with this client's case and knew it would be a terrific opportunity. However, she had a mandatory women's ministry meeting that she'd scheduled two weeks ago. She knew she couldn't miss it due to the nature of the meeting.

Shelly told her supervisor that she couldn't meet with the client that evening because of a prior commitment, but would be happy to meet with the client tomorrow. Barbara was livid. "You mean to tell me this client's case isn't important to you?" said Barbara in a sharp, mean, and aggressive voice. "I'm trying to help you build your clientele by giving you a high-profile case that will pay off big and you're turning it down!"

"No, Ms. Barbara, I'm not turning it down, I just can't meet her tonight," said Shelly, startled at her supervisor's response. "I already made another commitment two weeks ago that is just as important to me." At this point, Ms. Barbara's attitude and tone of voice becomes even more offensive. "Well, if you can't meet this client tonight, I'll just give her to someone who can," snarled Barbara.

"Wait, Ms. Barbara," said Shelly. "Just stop and think. There has never been a time that I haven't tried to meet the conditions of the clients you've given me. I've always been at your beck and call when it comes to representing this firm. Please understand, I can't do it this time because of my prior commitment."

"I'm very upset right now; I can't talk to you any further about this," Barbara snapped. "I have to go so I can think about this some more. I need to meet with you in my office before you leave." Then she hung up on Shelly.

A morning that had started out so peacefully turned into an upsetting, disturbing afternoon. Shelly's supervisor totally negated all the prior help and hard work Shelly put into the firm since day one just because she couldn't meet a client that evening. "How could she have responded that way?" Shelly thought. "She knows my predicament. I haven't given her any reason to doubt my work ethics or my ability to get the job done. Yet just because I can't meet the client tonight, she has an attitude about it, and out of spite she's going to give the client to another person."

With her mind in turmoil, Shelly took this situation to God in prayer.

She began to pray, "Father, show Ms. Barbara the error of her ways in this situation. There was no reason for her to get upset about this. I pray that you will change her attitude and that she'll be reasonable and calm about this whole situation. Let your peace reign. When I go into her office, I pray that you would have smoothed everything out and we will be able to reach an understanding peacefully and show respect toward each other. In Jesus' name, amen."

Later that day, Shelly nervously walked into Barbara's office. She felt uncomfortable and ready to defend herself, just like a typical lawyer. She wasn't sure what Barbara was going to do or say to her face to face.

As Barbara began to speak, however, it was as if she were another woman. Shelly knew God had done it. He had answered her prayers! Barbara was like a totally different person. Her tone of voice was pleasant, just like an instrument that was perfectly in tune with the rest of the band. Her choice of words was respectful, as if she'd reflected upon all that Shelly had given to her in previous situations. She also showed respect for Shelly's contributions. Because of Shelly's fervent prayer prior to the meeting, the two women were able to reach an understanding. Barbara gave the case to Shelly and the client agreed to meet Shelly on a more convenient day.

So often when we're passionate about something, we lose control of our mouths as we try to control the outcome of the situation.

Look up the following scriptures and pull a "key" from the scripture that will help you understand how we are to talk to people. Explain.

Philippians 2:5-8:

Proverbs 13:3

Proverbs 21:23

Exodus 4:12

Exodus 4:16

Moments of Reflection:

1. I want you to think back to a time when someone spoke to you in a tone that made you feel worthless. What keys would you use to speak "life" into yourself?

2. What will you do to ensure that the tone of your words are in tune with the tone of Christ?

Pray and meditate on these scriptures:

James 1:26 – If any man among you seems to be religious and bridled not his tongue, but deceived his own heart, this man's religion is vain.

I Peter 3:10 – For he that will love life and see good days, let him refrain his tongue from evil and his lips that they speak no guile.

Proverbs 23:7-8 – For as he thinketh in his heart, so is he: Eat and drink, saith he to thee; but his heart is not with thee. For the morsel which thou have eaten shalt thou vomit up, and lose thy sweet words.

Chapter 8

One Woman's Story

One Saturday night at 7:45, life changed forever. Earlier that week my husband asked if we could have a date night. I was so excited. Due to the issues of life, we hadn't been able to love on each other in a long time.

My husband was larger than life. A pillar in the community, he traveled with the movers and shakers. But despite his stellar public reputation, our marriage suffered behind the scenes. We had experienced deep breaches of trust. Several years ago, my husband brought home a child he'd conceived with another woman and told me this was now our child. The girl, Tammy, was 10 years old with a lot of attitude. She innocently clung to her daddy and eyed me with suspicion.

Everybody in our community knew about this situation. In fact, people in our neighborhood knew about Tammy long before I did because my husband traveled around town with Tammy.

As Tammy grew, I felt that she treated me disrespectfully. No one but her daddy could discipline her. My oldest daughter accepted Tammy; however, my other three children struggled tremendously with how Tammy interacted with me.

Occasionally, Tammy's mother would come to visit her at my home. Her presence was another slap in the face to my children and me. Because others in the community knew about this embarrassing situation, I couldn't share my feelings with anyone. I shut down emotionally.

But back to the date night: I was excited because this could spark a new beginning for my husband, our four children we had together, and me. The children had felt the tension and stress in our home as they were growing up. I'd been so embarrassed that I had to introduce this child to my other children. I felt less than a woman because my children looked at me as if they felt sorry for me. However, I made sure that all the children were ready for school. I cared for the home front and worked hard every day. Even though the children were a little older now, I still could see the pain of the betrayal in their eyes. I could see how hurt they were. Maybe this was the answer to all of our prayers.

My husband came home that evening with a dozen red roses. He was a very romantic man. He had music playing. We looked into each other's eyes and felt connected. I felt warm and ready to forgive everything he'd ever done to me. I wanted to believe he had changed. I felt like a woman. I felt desired.

We talked about old times, the good old days, all of our friends. How blessed we had been through the years, how beautiful our children were. Toward the latter part of the evening we found ourselves in each other's arms. Then he put on the CD, "Everything Must Change." I was sure this meant we were making a new start. I was elated.

After the song was over, as I lay in his arms, he lifted me up, we looked in each other's eyes, and he romantically explained why he needed a divorce.

I was still floating on Cloud 9, so his words made no sense. I asked him to say that again. He repeated it: He needed a divorce. He no longer desired to be with me. I was devastated. I felt betrayed, set up, and worthless. How could I be so stupid? How could I have trusted this man again?

He left the house. I cried, and cried, and cried. I couldn't come out of my room for days. Upon getting myself together, I struggled with where to turn. Because of my total commitment to my husband and family, there was not a friend to whom I felt close enough to trust my shattered emotions. I chose to die. My soul (mind, will, and emotions) died that day.

Now that I am an old woman, I often reflect on the day I died and the years that passed me by because of my internal pain. I wish I could have called someone who would have spoken into my life in a way that would have saved my soul. If I would have talked to the wrong person, I could have killed my husband. I didn't trust anyone else with this brokenness. As a result, I lived in a prison. I lost 20 years of my life not being able to find a reason to enjoy the gift of life.

Address the issues that you see in this scenario (such as unforgiveness, shame, or bitterness) and speak life to them.

1. How could you have encouraged this woman to love herself?

2. If this woman had trusted you to save her life, what would you have said to her?

3. After reading your response, were you able to speak life to this woman? Why or why not?

4. How would you point this woman to a life of freedom?

Moments of Reflection:

1. Think of a time when you felt that your spouse or a previous boy-friend was cheating on you. Did you want to hear the truth? How did you want to hear the truth? Encourage yourself in this type of situation.

2. What will you do to ensure that you'll be prepared to speak "life" into a sister- friend who shares with you that her husband/boyfriend is cheating?

Pray and meditate on these scriptures:

Proverbs 18:15 – The heart of the prudent acquires knowledge, and the ear of the wise seeks knowledge.

Ephesians 4:29 – Let no corrupt communication proceed out of your mouth, but what is good for necessary edification, that it may impart grace to the hearers.

Proverbs 4:23 – Keep thy heart with all diligence; for out of it are the issues of life.

Enter the Splendor
of the
Tea Room

Chapter 9

The Ministry is in Your Mouth

Welcome

to the Tea Room

where

the ministry is in your mouth

and

the splendor of the

tea room

is in you!

Splendor n. 1 great luster or brightness; brilliance 2 magnificent richness or glory; pomp, grandeur

What is the Splendor of the Tea Room?

The Tea Room is a grassroots effort that teaches individuals how to speak life and bring light into dark situations. Through this nationwide movement, I'm challenging men and women to banish the blues and take decisive action when family and friends experience difficult situations. Those willing to enter the Tea Room will learn how to speak purposefully and share their own experiences to help others in their circle of influence.

If you typically respond to trouble with negative comments, gloomy words, or gossip, you need to take a trip to the Tea Room.

When we hear that something has happened to a loved one, we often say, "Get over it." Or we say things like, "Did you hear so-and-so has AIDS? Stay away from that house!" We don't need to gossip. We need to listen and learn what we can do to step in and help our friends, relatives, and neighbors through this trauma.

In the inviting, soothing atmosphere of the Tea Room, we'll learn how to speak purposefully and share our experiences to help others. After years of simply crying over our problems, you and your family members can come together at the kitchen table or living-room sofa and begin addressing problems in word and deed. As a family, you and your loved ones will take action and speak in a way that brings life. You'll gain the ability to speak, pray, share, send cards or do whatever is necessary so that negative events don't overcome your entire family.

Cups Running Over

We sponsored the first Tea Room in College Park, Maryland, late last year. Soothing tea and soul-stirring words greeted more than 50 women during a special event designed to give women a chance to relax and reminisce as they learned the importance of speaking life into their circles of influence.

Tea Room participants had an opportunity to share stories about the teacups they brought with them to the event. One woman brought a cup that belonged to her great-grandmother. Two other teacups were at least 50 years old. Shortly thereafter, the women enjoyed tea, coffee, and light refreshments in front of a roaring fire. The tea offered a rare opportunity for busy, overextended women to relax, fellowship and even shop from vendors in a calm, tasteful setting.

Idle chitchat over tea turned into a serious discussion about speaking light into dark situations when I gave my keynote address on "Making Your Mouth a Ministry." Using personal, intimate stories from my own life, I challenged the women to intentionally reach out to others in their circles of influence -- including family members, neighbors, or co-workers -- who might be facing grief, loss, divorce, abuse, or emotional scars. Women can respond proactively by speaking, praying, counseling, sending cards, or doing whatever they need to do so that negative events will not overcome entire families.

Joining the Movement

At the end of the event, I challenged participants to become ambassadors for their circles of influence. These ambassadors will receive training in how to speak and serve their families and friends during times of crisis. I encouraged the ambassadors to conduct teas in their own homes, using the book Make Your Mouth a Ministry as a discussion topic. Those who learn how to speak life eventually will begin to teach others how to do the same.

The ambassadors will meet regularly to share testimonies of how they're changing their homes, jobs, and communities. After all, the

Tea Room is in you, and the ministry is in your mouth.

Join us as we answer the call to speak life!

Mrs. Deborah Leaner

Chapter 10

It's Tea Time
The Book Club

Welcome To "My Cup of Tea"

Through Make Your Mouth a Ministry, you have an opportunity to help others equip themselves to speak life into others. "My Cup of Tea" allows you to host a tea in your home and share this life-changing message with your circle of influence.

Together we can cast down low self-esteem and rise to esteem others, create energy that breathes life in dark situations, and change the atmosphere around us by making a commitment to "make your mouth a ministry."

Listed below are four requirements:

1. Say "YES" to a life-changing opportunity by participating in a Circle of Influence Gathering (CIG).

2. Become an Ambassador.

3. Host a Circle of Influence Gathering Tea.

4. Be an advocate for making your mouth a ministry by participating in the CIG Challenge.

1. I say "YES!"

Congratulations!

2. Become an Ambassador.

Make Your Mouth A Ministry ambassadors are a select group of individuals who have accepted the call and made a conscious commitment to speak life to their circle of influence. As an ambassador, you have become part of a unique network of individuals who have chosen to be agents of change by spreading the message "Speak Life."

3. Host a Circle of Influence Gathering.

Who is My Circle of Influence?

Your Circle of Influence (CIG) includes everyone to whom you're connected. Your circle may include book club participants, business networks, church members, community and civic groups, co-workers, family, friends, neighbors, sister-friends, fraternity/sorority members, teachers, healthcare providers, lawyers, your postmaster, daycare providers, your barber, day spa providers, hair and nail technicians, your exercise partner, and so on. Anyone you connect with in your personal and professional life is part of your circle of influence.

What is a Circle of Influence Gathering (Tea)?

The purpose of the gathering is to challenge your guests to resurrect the latent power that lies in their mouths. They will strengthen the muscle needed to speak life into dark situations by reading and discussing the book Make Your Mouth A Ministry.

Ambassadors and guests will generally meet monthly (your choice) to read and interact with each other as they learn to address darkness in their lives, empower others to speak life, and connect each other to the power of unity within the circle.

4. Learn more about the challenge in the "Speak Life not Death" section of this book.

Attached is a letter that I received from an ambassador. This ambassador hosted a Tea and Talk, which represents "My Cup of Tea."

Ladies,

I'd like to thank those of you who were able to join me last Saturday. I had a great time and was very excited to share my commitment with you. For those of you who weren't able to make it, I don't want you to miss this great opportunity for growth.

Last week, I shared that I've been given the opportunity to help other women equip themselves to speak life into other people. I played a CD with excerpts from a book called Make Your Mouth a Ministry by Deborah Leaner. I met Mrs. Leaner in November 2007 and was introduced to her ministry. Her ministry was birthed out of the loss of her son, Korey, to cancer when he was just 33 years old.

As Mrs. Leaner went through her son's illness, she and her family encountered many challenges. As they and others tried to come to grips with Korey's illness, they found that people didn't know what to say or do. Some acted as if he weren't ill. Some made hurtful and discouraging comments. Some stayed away. Deborah was there with Korey and encouraged him along the way. Deborah prayed for and talked to her son. Korey asked his mother to write a book to help others to be the strength the she had been for him. Thus Make Your Mouth a Ministry was born.

Mrs. Leaner's ministry is helping to equip people just like us to be a light in people's dark situations. It isn't always death, but it may be struggles with children, difficulties in marriage, illness, pressures at work, caring for aging parents -- the list goes on and on. We need to be equipped to speak life and to give a lifeline to those who are in our circle. Mrs. Leaner is traveling around the country and hosting teas to share her vision. The idea is that people will host teas in their homes and share this message with their circles of influence. Each of you is a part of my circle of influence. Our circle of influence includes our family, friends, co-workers, church members, and sorority members -- anyone with whom we come in contact. Each of us has our own circle of influence.

As part of the tea, we'll read the book and use the information to prepare ourselves to help others in our lives. Once we've been equipped, I hope that some of you will desire to have teas to equip people in your circle of influence so we can continue to duplicate this effort.

It appeared that several of you were interested in making your mouth a ministry. The idea is that we would meet monthly and cover two to three chapters. It should take three to four months to complete the book. I will host the teas at my home and we can decide on a Saturday that works for all.

The book will be available in April. However, we don't want to lose momentum. In that regard, Mrs. Leaner suggested and I am requesting that through the month of March, we keep a journal of when we made our mouths a ministry and when we didn't. We'll get together in March to share our successes and to discuss the challenges that we faced. Please let me know this week if you're interested in making the commitment to make your mouth a ministry.

Session One

Allow 2 hours and 15 minutes for this session.

Greeting and ice breaker.

15 minutes

My Cup of Tea

30 minutes
Serve your choice of tea as you
share with your guests why you've
invited them to "My Cup of Tea" and why
you made the commitment.

It's Tea Time

60 minutes
Discovering the flavor of tea in the mouths of your guests.

Scented Tea
15 minutes
Smelling the aroma of the tea in you (life application).

Closing
15 minutes

The next pages contain recommended formats for Ambassadors of Make Your Mouth A Ministry to use when you host your Circle of Influence gatherings. The sessions outlined in the tea cup are guidelines you can use to present "MY CUP OF TEA!"

Welcome To My Cup of Tea

Step One: 15 minutes - Greeting and ice breaker

Welcome your guests with a smile as you greet them at the front door. Lead them to the tea room in your home and introduce each guest. Let them know that you're excited about telling them how your life has been transformed by the Tea Room.

Prepare for the ice breaker by ensuring that you've created an atmosphere that allows guests to feel free to share.

Ice Breakers

• Name two strong, positive characteristics about each person you invited and share it with the group.

• Go around the room and ask each guest to share with the group two things they like to do after a stressful day.

- Write the names of your guests on small pieces of paper and place the names in a hat. Ask your guests to pick a name. The person who has been picked must describe her day or week. If the day or week has been difficult, the guest who selected her name will try to offer encouragement (speak life).

My Cup of Tea

Step Two: 30 minutes

Serving tea should be reminiscent of the times when "women of old" would get together, serve tea, and talk about what was going on in the home or in the community. Share with your friends and loved ones why you've invited them to your "cup of tea."

Share with the ladies as you serve the tea. Pour each lady's tea and talk so that everyone feels your compassion and sees your level of commitment for how and why this transformation happened in your life. Let them know that you would like for them to listen to a CD. The CD lasts about 10 minutes.

It's Tea Time!

Step Three: 60 minutes - Discovering the flavor of tea in the mouths of your guests

This is the time to listen to your guests. The CD will resurrect some thoughts in the minds and hearts of your guests and they'll want to share. At this point just listen and perhaps take some mental notes so that you can speak to how this book will help with the issues of life being discussed. This is the time to see if any of the ladies would like to take this journey with you. If so, they must do the following:

- Sign a charge to work toward speaking life to their circle of influence (the charge is included in the Ambassador's Kit).
- They should receive an assignment from the Ambassador to journal daily for the next two weeks to assess if they're speaking life on a daily basis.
- They should order their books within the next two weeks and be prepared to discuss the introduction and chapter one through three. Set the date for the next meeting. Remind the ladies to bring their books to the next meeting along with their two weeks' journal assignment.

Scented Tea

Step Four: 15 minutes - Smelling the aroma of the tea in you.
Within three minutes share a story that supports the importance of

speaking life into yourself and or others.

Closing

Step Five: 15 minutes

Once you have the information you need, move to the closing with a quick prayer, then get your guests' coats or begin to walk them to the door. It is very important that your guests know that this gathering was about "your cup of tea" and your tea gathering will be timely and purposeful. If someone wants to talk to you about something else, schedule another time to meet with her on a one-on-one basis.

Session Two

Allow 2 hours and 15 minutes for this session.

Greeting

10 minutes

My Cup of Tea

35 minutes
Serve your choice of tea and discuss the journal assignment.

It's Tea Time!

60 minutes
Review chapter one and discuss the introduction to the book and chapter two and three entitled, "Speaking Life as a Spiritual Calling" and "Your Mouth Ain't No River, But It Will Surely Drown You."

Scented Tea

15 minutes
Smelling the aroma of the tea in the mouths of your guests.

Closing

15 minutes

Greeting

Step One: 10 minutes

Welcome your guests with a smile as you greet them at the front
door. Lead them to the tea room in your home. Let them know that
you're excited and grateful that they've chosen to equip themselves
to help their circle of influence with the issues of life through reading this book.

My Cup of Tea

Step Two: 35 minutes

Remember that serving tea should be reminiscent of the times when
"women of old" would get together, serve tea, and talk about what
was going on in the home or in the community.

It's now time for you to share the results of your journaling experiences. Be honest and transparent so you'll create an atmosphere
that allows the members of your circle of influence to speak their
hearts.

Share with the ladies as you serve the tea. Pour each lady's tea
and talk so that every woman feels your sincerity, commitment, and
passion about the outcome of your journaling experience. Then en-

courage each person to share with the group her experience with journaling during the last two weeks.

It's Tea Time!

Step Three: 60 minutes

Review chapter one and discuss the introduction to the book as well as chapters two and three. Each person should be able to share her heart and know that this is a safe place for discussion.

Scented Tea

Step Four: 15 minutes - Smelling the aroma of the tea in the mouths of your guests.

Discuss any unique opportunities presented to you to speak life into someone else's life since you last met.

Closing

Step Five: 15 minutes

Announce the date of the next meeting. Ask them to read chapter four, entitled, "101 Ways to Speak Life," as well as the introduction and the first principle in the Tool Kit, entitled, "A Christ-Centered Heart." Once you've given your guests their assignment for the next meeting, you should move quickly to the closing with a quick prayer, then get their coats or begin to walk them to the door. It is very important that your guests know that this gathering was about "your cup of tea" and your tea gathering will be timely and purpose-ful. If someone wants to talk with you about something else, please schedule another time to meet with her on a one-on-one basis.

Session Three

Allow 2 hours and 15 minutes for this session.

Greeting

10 minutes

My Cup of Tea

35 minutes

Serve your choice of tea and discuss your personal experience as a result of reading chapter four, entitled, "101 Ways to Speak Life," as well as the introduction to the Tool Kit along with the first principle, entitled, "A Christ-Centered Heart."

It's Tea Time!

60 minutes
Discuss chapter four, the introduction, and the first principle in the Tool Kit.

Scented Tea

15 minutes
Smelling the aroma of the tea in the mouths of your guests.

Closing

15 minutes

Greeting

Step One: 10 minutes

Welcome your guests with a smile as you greet them at the front door. Lead them to the tea room in your home. Begin to speak life to them through one of the characteristics used in principle one of the Tool Kit.

My Cup of Tea

Step Two: 35 minutes

Remember that serving tea should be reminiscent of the times when "women of old" would get together, serve tea, and talk about what was going on in the home or in the community. (Make it fun -- dress up like the "women of old.")

It's now time for you to share the results of your experience with chapter four as well as the introduction and the first principle in the Tool Kit. Be honest and transparent so you'll create an atmosphere that allows the members of your circle of influence to speak their hearts.

Share with the ladies as you serve the tea. Pour each lady's tea and talk so that everyone feels your sincerity and passion as you share the outcomes of this assignment.

It's Tea Time!

Step Three: 60 minutes

Discuss chapter four as well as the introduction and the first principle, entitled, "A Christ-Centered Heart" of the Tool Kit. Each person should be able to share her heart and know that this is a safe place for discussion.

Scented Tea

Step Four: 15 minutes   Smelling the aroma of the tea in the mouths of your guests.

Discuss any unique opportunities presented to you to speak life to someone else since you last met.

Closing

Step Five: 15 Minutes

Announce the date of the next meeting. Ask your guests to read chapters five and six of the book and the second principle in the Tool Kit, entitled, "Affirming Yourself Through the Word of God."

Once you've given your guests their assignment for the next meeting, you should move to the closing with a quick prayer, then get their coats or begin to walk them to the door. It is very important that your guests know that this gathering was about "your cup of tea" and your tea gathering will be timely and purposeful. If someone wants to talk with you about something else, please schedule another time to meet with her on a one-on-one basis.

Session Four

Allow 2 hours and 15 minutes for this session.

Greeting

10 minutes

My Cup of Tea

35 minutes
Serve your choice of tea and discuss your personal experiences as a result of reading chapters five and six, entitled, "Refreshing Water Spa" and "Meeting in the Ladies' Room" along with the second principle in the Tool Kit, entitled, "Affirming Yourself Through the Word of God."

It's Tea Time
60 minutes
Discuss chapters five, six, and the second principle in the Tool Kit.

Scented Tea

15 minutes
Smelling the aroma of the tea in the mouths of your guests.

Closing
15 minutes

Greeting

Step One: 10 minutes- Greeting

Welcome your guests with a smile as you greet them at the front door. Lead them to the tea room in your home. Begin to speak life to them by expressing one of the characteristics used in the second principle of the Tool Kit.

My Cup of Tea

Step Two: 35 minutes

Remember that serving tea should be reminiscent of the times when "women of old" would get together, serve tea, and talk about what was going on in the home or in the community. (Make it fun -- dress up like the "women of old.")

It's now time for you to share the outcome of your experience with chapters five and six, entitled, "Refreshing Water Spa" and "Meeting in the Ladies' Room" along with the second principle in the Tool Kit, entitled, "Affirming Yourself Through the Word of God." Be honest and transparent so you'll create an atmosphere that allows the members of your circle of influence to speak their hearts.

 Share with the ladies as you serve the tea. Pour each lady's tea and talk so that everyone feels your sincerity and passion as you share the outcomes of this assignment.

It's Tea Time!

Step Three: 60 mintues

Discuss chapters five and six entitled, "Refreshing Water Spa" and "Meeting in the Ladies' Room" along with the second principle in the Tool Kit, entitled, "Affirming Yourself Through the Word." Each person should be able to share her heart and know that this is a safe place for discussion.

Scented Tea

Step Four: 15 minutes   Smelling the aroma of the tea in the mouths of your guests.

Discuss any unique opportunities presented to you to speak life to someone else since you last met.

Closing

Step Five: 15 Minutes

Announce the date of the next meeting. Ask your guests to read chapters seven and eight, entitled, "Tune Your Tone" and "One Woman's Story" along with the third principle in the Tool Kit, entitled, "Cultivate a Heart of Humility."

Once you've given your guests their assignment for the next meeting, you should move to the closing with a quick prayer, then get their coats or begin to walk them to the door. It is very important that your guests know that this gathering was about "your cup of tea" and your tea gathering will be timely and purposeful. If someone wants to talk with you about something else, please schedule another time to meet with her on a one-on-one basis.

Session Five

Allow 2 hours and 15 minutes for this session.

Greeting

10 minutes

It's Tea Time

35 minutes
Serve your choice of tea and discuss chapter seven and eight entitled, "Tune Your Tone" and "One Woman's Story," along with the third principle in the Tool Kit, entitled, "Cultivate a Heart of Humility."

My Cup of Tea

60 minutes
Discuss chapter seven and eight and the third principle in the Tool Kit.

Scented Tea

15 minutes
Smelling the aroma of the tea in the mouths of your guests.

Closing

15 minutes

Greeting

Step One: 10 minutes- Greeting

Welcome your guests with a smile as you greet them at the front door. Lead them to the tea room in your home. Begin to speak life to them through expressing one of the characteristics of the third principle in the Tool Kit.

My Cup of Tea

Step Two: 35 minutes

Remember that serving tea should be reminiscent of the times when "women of old" would get together, serve tea, and talk about what was going on in the home or in the community. (Make it fun -- dress up like the "women of old.")

It's now time for you to share the results of your experiences with chapters seven and eight and the third principle in the Tool Kit. Be honest and transparent so you'll create an environment that allows the members of your circle of influence to speak their hearts.

Share with the ladies as you serve the tea. Pour each lady's tea and talk so that everyone feels your sincerity and passion.

It's Tea Time!

Step Three: 60 minutes

Discuss chapters seven and eight, entitled, "Tune Your Tone" and "One Woman's Story" along with the third principle in the Tool Kit entitled, "Cultivate a Heart of Humility." Each person should be able to share her heart and know that this is a safe place for discussion.

Scented Tea

Step Four: 15 minutes - Smelling the aroma of the tea in the mouths of your guests.

Discuss any unique opportunities presented to you to speak life to someone else since you last met.

Closing

Step Five: 15 minutes

Announce the date of the next meeting. Ask them to read principle four, five, and six in the Tool Kit, entitled, "Interceding for Others," "Encouraging Yourself," and "Speaking the Truth in Love." Explain that you'll introduce the SPEAK "LIFE" NOT "DEATH" challenge.

Once you've given your guests their assignment for the next meeting, you should move to the closing with a quick prayer, then get their coats or begin to walk them to the door. It is very important that your guests know that this gathering was about "your cup of tea" and your tea gathering will be timely and purposeful. If someone wants to talk with you, please schedule another time to meet with her on a one-on-one basis.

Chapter 11

The Make Your Mouth a Ministry Challenge

Speak "Life" not "Death"

Join the 30-Day Challenge

and

"Make Your Mouth

a Ministry"

For Your
Circle of Influence
Gathering

AMBASSADOR'S CHALLENGE

Deborah Leaner, author of Make Your Mouth a Ministry, and your ambassador invite you to take the 30-Day Challenge and "Make Your Mouth a Ministry." The challenge is a resounding call to Circle of Influence Gathering participants across the country, encouraging you to use your mouth to speak "life" and not "death" in the lives of others.

By participating in this extraordinary, life-changing event, you'll commit to these objectives:

- Align Your Mouth with a Christ-Centered Heart
- Affirm Others
- Cultivate a Heart of Humility
- Intercede for Others in Prayer
- Encourage Yourself
- Speak the Truth in Love

Don't Delay—"Make Your Mouth A Ministry" TODAY!

The Purpose:

Based on her book Make Your Mouth A Ministry, Deborah Leaner presents an opportunity for ordinary people who want God to use them in extraordinary ways in the lives of others. Transformation will take place through the power of the Holy Spirit. Indeed, as you "make your mouth a ministry," you'll witness the power of the breath of life as it does the work of turning around low self-esteem, lying lips, broken hearts, pressures at work, drama in our churches, difficult marriages, and more!

The Challenge:

Join Deborah and the Make Your Mouth A Ministry Team for an extraordinary 30-Day Challenge as they spread the call across the country to "make your mouth a ministry." The challenge will assess how well you're applying the six principles in the Make Your Mouth A Ministry Tool Kit section of the book.

- Align Your Mouth with a Christ-Centered Heart
- Affirm Others
- Cultivate a Heart of Humility
- Intercede for Others in Prayer

- Encourage Yourself
- Speak the Truth in Love

AMBASSADOR'S CHALLENGE

You will find the Circle of Influence Gathering structure for the challenge in the Ambassador's Kit.

Why participate?

This is a call for everyone to use words in a powerful manner by speaking "life" into themselves as well as others. Our mouth is home to a powerful tool, our tongue. During this challenge, you'll learn to encourage yourself and others, intercede for others in prayer, and speak truth in love. You'll then be ready to speak "life" and not "death" in everyday circumstances and situations.

The Impact:

Have you heard the expression "you are what you speak"? Every day we plant seeds of "life" or "death" with our mouths. We impact our daily lives and the lives of others with the words we speak. Not only are we affected, but our words also play a role in the way we respond to others and individuals respond to us. We're often unaware of the harm our words can cause.

How do you use your mouth? What words do you speak to your children, co-workers, families, spouses, friends, and leaders? How often do you really think before you speak? What impact do your words have on others?

Speak "Life" not "Death"
Join the 30-Day Challenge
and
"Make Your Mouth
a Ministry"

For Churches and Organizations

Deborah Leaner, author of Make Your Mouth a Ministry, invites you and your organization to take the 30-Day Challenge and "make your mouth a ministry." The challenge is a resounding call to use your mouth to speak "life" and not "death" in the lives of others.

By participating in this extraordinary, life-changing event, you'll commit to these objectives:

• Align Your Mouth with a Christ-Centered Heart
• Affirm Others
• Cultivate a Heart of Humility
• Intercede for Others in Prayer
• Encourage Yourself
• Speak the Truth in Love

Don't Delay—Join the challenge

and "Make Your Mouth A Ministry" TODAY!

The Purpose:

Based on her book Make Your Mouth A Ministry, Deborah Leaner presents an opportunity to stir up the latent power in the mouths of ordinary people who want God to use them in extraordinary ways in the lives of others. Transformation will take place through the power of the Holy Spirit; indeed, you'll witness the power of the breath of life as it does the work of turning around low self-esteem, lying lips, broken hearts, pressures at work, drama in our churches, difficult marriages, and more!

The Challenge:

Join Deborah and the Make Your Mouth A Ministry Team for an extraordinary 30-day nationwide challenge to "make your mouth a ministry." The challenge will assess how well you're applying the six principles in the Make Your Mouth A Ministry Tool Kit section of the book.

- Align Your Mouth with a Christ-Centered Heart
- Affirm Others
- Cultivate a Heart of Humility
- Intercede for Others in Prayer
- Encourage Yourself
- Speak the Truth in Love

For Organizations, Churches, and Businesses

Organizations, churches, and businesses should allow their members and/or employees 30 days to read the six principles found in the Tool Kit section of the book. After reading the assignment, teams of two to six people (small groups) will commit during the next 30 days to be accountable for the six principles they read in the Tool Kit. At the end of the challenge, team members will participate in a debriefing and discuss their experiences around the principles and share a characteristic from that principle that affected their individual lives as well as others.

Each team will consist of a captain and members. Teams will interact with one another and be accountable to each other during the 30-Day Challenge. Each team will sign a team charge to demonstrate commitment for the next 30 days of the challenge.

Why participate?

This is a call for everyone to use words in a powerful manner by speaking "life" into themselves as well as others. Your mouth is home to a powerful tool, your tongue. During this challenge, you'll learn to encourage yourself and others, intercede for others in prayer, and speak truth in love. You'll then be ready to speak "life" and not "death" in everyday circumstances and situations.

The Impact:

Have you heard the expression "you are what you speak"? Every day we plant seeds of "life" or "death" with our mouths. We impact our daily lives and the lives of others with the words we speak. Not only are we affected, but our words also play a role in the way we respond to others and individuals respond to us. We're often unaware of the harm our words can cause.

How do you use your mouth? What words do you speak to your children, co-workers, families, spouses, friends, and leaders? How often do you really think before you speak? What impact do your words have on others?

Who should join?

Everyone who's willing to commit and take powerful steps to "make your mouth a ministry." So invite your family, friends, girlfriends, sister-friends, co-workers, neighbors, community, church, and social organizations to participate in the Make Your Mouth A Ministry 30-Day Challenge. This awesome experience will change your life and what you speak.

How do I join?

1. Develop your team of two to six people.

2. Go to www.deborahleaner.com, click on MYMAM, and download the pre-challenge workshop.

3. Fill out the challenge form.

4. Commit to the next 30 days by signing the team charge.

When do I get started?

Read the six principles found in the Tool Kit section of Make Your Mouth A Ministry, then download the pre-challenge workshop. Complete the enclosed challenge form and return it to your team captain. Or fill out the form online and we'll pair you with others in your area who would like to take the challenge.

Make Your Mouth a Ministry
Challenge Guidelines

Please adhere to the following guidelines during the next 30 days.

- The challenge will continue for 30 days.

- Teams will meet after reading the book for a pre-challenge workshop.

- Participants will record their experiences in the Speak Life Journal included in the book.

- Teams should consist of two to six people, including a captain and members.

- Participants must review the guidelines and sign the charge to demonstrate their commitment to the 30-Day Challenge.

- Upon completion of the challenge, teams will share their experiences and celebrate.

- Team captain will coach members and keep them on track throughout the 30-Day Challenge.

- After the challenge is over, we encourage you to reach out to others and teach them to speak life so that the process will continue and we can all speak life into each other.

30 ~ Day Challenge
Make Your Mouth A Ministry

TEAM ACCOUNTABILITY LOG

Team Name:_____

Team Captain:_____

WEEK_____

PART IV

Make Your Mouth A Ministry Tool Kit

Introduction

"Make Your Mouth a Ministry" has produced a tool kit that will inspire, empower, and connect you with methods to ensure that the words coming out of your mouth generate a wealth of power in your life and the lives of others.

Only God speaks the creating power of life *(John 1:1 states that "In the beginning was the Word, and the Word was with God, and the Word was God).* These tools will help you tap into that supernatural power given to you by the Holy Spirit. When we're sensitive to the teachings of the Holy Spirit, we speak blessings, share life lessons, give praise and thanksgiving, give voice to a gracious greeting, pray with and for others, laugh out loud, comfort a friend, paint wonderful words of encouragement, and speak a word from the Lord… just to name a few.

Luke 21:15 make it clear that we've been given *"a mouth and wisdom which all your adversaries will not be able to contradict or resist."* Using the wisdom and understanding given by the Holy Spirit, God can use us to empower others and influence the way they act, think, respond, initiate, and make decisions that will affect any given area of their lives. God can use our mouths for ministry.

This is a powerful responsibility if you're disconnected from the guidance of the Holy Spirit; however, for those who are connected to the power of the Holy Spirit, this is an awesome opportunity and privilege. God uses us to change the lives of others, welcome new people into our circles of influence, and walk in our destiny.

We start this process by addressing your circle of influence. In this book, your circle of influence includes people you can empower and influence.

Second, this book includes nuts and bolts, which will help you succeed as you connect with others. When you apply these nuts and bolts appropriately, you'll establish a foundation that will prepare you, move you, and push you into your ministry, clearly motivated by love.

To help you create an environment that breeds life, empowers others, and connects you with others, we've developed six principles you can use to control what comes out of your mouth. By mastering these principles, you'll be well on your way to making your mouth a ministry, the bridge to your destiny.

Each principle offers assessments, confessions, daily calendar/journal items, supportive scriptures, tips to seeking godly counsel, lists of relative resources, and accountability tools.

Understanding and Identifying Your Circle of Influence

When I say circle of influence, I'm not talking about the things around you that have an effect on you and your life. Rather, I'm speaking of the people and things around you and your life that you have the power to influence.

Tons of teachings exist that deal with the importance of being aware of and maintaining control over your circle of influence; that is, your friends, and other people with whom you associate. We address that same circle of influence in this book, but we focus on the influence that you have on them.

Below is a diagram that will aid you in identifying your circle of influence. Research says that everyone influences someone.

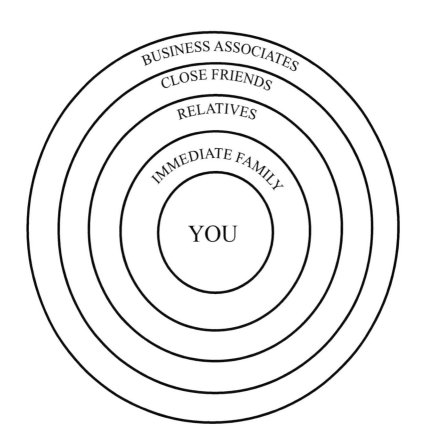

The Nuts and Bolts

Before you can begin to understand the wealth of power in your mouth, you must learn a few fundamentals.

First, AWARENESS: Always be aware of the awesome power God has created in your mouth. In our daily lives we tell our children to always pay attention to their surroundings. This is exactly what God is telling us (His children) about the awesome power He has placed in our mouths. This power creates your surroundings, changes the atmosphere around you, aligns destinies with His will, resurrects dead lives, provides living water in dry places, and brings light to darkness. Testimonies have come forward as examples of how His word has given sight to the blind, turned on deaf ears, healed broken hearts, and given beauty for ashes. All of this happens through the awesome power God has created in our mouths.

Proverbs 18:21 says that "Death and life are in the power of the tongue: and they that love it shall eat the fruit thereof." This means that the words that come out of your mouth, good or bad, will determine the outcome (fruit) that will govern your life. In other words, your life follows your words. *Matthew 12:34 says, "out of the*

ABUNDANCE OF THE HEART the mouth speaketh." This simply means that the condition of your heart will dictate what comes out of your mouth. We'll deal later with the processes associated with the various conditions of the heart -- why your heart is in the shape that it's in and how to have a heart transformation.

Second, RECOGNIZE/ IDENTIFY when the spirit of darkness attempts to consume and destroy you, your family, and your surroundings. CALL HIM OUT! *Ephesians 6:12 tells us, "For we wrestle not against flesh and blood, but against principalities, against powers, against the rulers of the darkness of this world, against spiritual wickedness in high places."*

You must understand that our enemy isn't flesh and blood. Our enemy isn't people! We wrestle with an evil spirit sometimes traveling in an earthly vessel. For example, when women join the discipleship ministry I developed, they often say, "Mrs. Deborah, I can't trust women; therefore, this experience will be difficult because I want nothing to do with women." In response, I present the truth (God's word) about how our spirit can plug into His spirit and how we can free ourselves from dark places (struggle). Further, I show them how to love on their sisters in a way that they've never learned. As a result, their hearts and words change.

Third, EQUIP yourself for the calling. You're already a winner, so accept it and equip yourself to move forward in the kingdom and do what God has called you to do (destiny). In my experience, the hardest thing to do is to believe that God really wants to use you. Because of our disbelief, we never prepare ourselves for the calling.

THIS IS MAJOR: You must accept your calling. Once you accept your calling, you must move toward your calling. In order to move

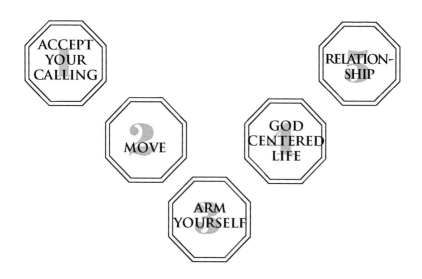

toward your calling, you must arm yourself. To prepare and equip yourself, God must be at the center of your life. Strengthen yourself daily by building a relationship with Christ, communicating with Him, studying His word to show yourself approved, accepting your place in the kingdom, and working to help others find their place in God's family. Before long, you will find yourself right in the middle of your destiny.

When you have the proper tools to succeed, the first thing you'll learn is that God wants to be in relationship with you.

Through your calling you'll learn from Him how to develop relationships by developing one with Him. Second, you'll learn how to communicate (pray) effectively with Him through His word. He will teach you when to speak and when to listen and meditate on His word. Acts 6:4 says, *"But we will give ourselves continually to prayer, and to the ministry of the word."*

When you arm yourself with just these weapons, God will prepare you to develop godly relationships (fellowship) through prayer partners, Christian fellowship, dating (equally yoked), effective communication with authorities in your life, new friends, and so on. *Romans 12:5* says, *"So we, being many, are one body in Christ, and every one members one of another."*

RESTORATION: Last, God said in the 23rd Psalm that He will restore YOUR SOUL.

Know that God loves you, and as you serve others, He will restore your soul (mind, will, and emotions). In the 23rd Psalm, David shares his own experience to show us how the Lord will restore His people. This psalm uses the Shepherd and sheep illustration to show us how we must position ourselves as sheep in Christ to have the protection, guidance, and provisions of the Good Shepherd.

From research, we know that sheep depend completely on the Shepherd for food, direction, and protection. In this illustration, we're the sheep and the Lord is the Shepherd. We must lean totally on our heavenly Father, the good Shepherd. When we get in position, He restores our souls as we minister to others.

The New Testament calls Jesus the Good Shepherd, the Great Shepherd, and the Chief Shepherd. He knows what is best for us; He will do right by us. He cares about every detail (the nuts and bolts) in our lives. He has the power of restoration and He said that He leads us beside the still waters and He restores our souls.

Six Principles of Making Your Mouth a Ministry

1. CHRIST-CENTERED HEART

2. AFFIRMATION

3. CULTIVATE THE HEART OF HUMILITY

4. INTERCEDE FOR OTHERS

5. ENCOURAGEMENT

6. SPEAK THE TRUTH IN LOVE

1. A CHRIST-CENTERED HEART: his principle symbolizes the heartbeat of God. A symbol is a real sign, something that represents something else. Of course, the heart is synonymous with love. However, it has many other associations, too. Here are just a few

examples:

- Have a heart - be merciful

- Change of heart - change your mind

- To know something by heart - memorize something

- Broken heart - to lose love

- Heartfelt - deeply felt

- Have your heart in the right place - to be kind

- Cry your heart out - to grieve

- Heavy heart - sadness

- Have your heart set on - to want something badly

- Open one's heart

- To give one's heart

When we speak of a Christ-centered heart, we're looking for evidence (fruit) that God's heartbeat is at the center of your heart. This is important because the issues of life flow from the heart of man (Proverbs 4:23). Your ministry will bless others when they see the heart of God through your interactions, especially when things don't seem to be in your favor.

These acts will be the mirror of your heart. In other words, you can't fake this. If your heart isn't Christ-centered, the words that flow from your mouth will represent the fruit of death.

Lesson: Stay connected to the word so you can bear fruit consistently.

Below are a few characteristics of a woman who has a Christ-centered heart. Her mouth, therefore, is ready for ministry.

- **Fruit of the spirit - Agape:** Love/compassion for all people; joy or steadfast delight; Peace and tranquility in the midst of the storms of life; Longsuffering demonstrated by waiting on the Lord and being of good courage; kindness and caring for others; goodness -- reaching out to do good even when others don't deserve such treatment; faithfulness and dependability; gentleness, shown by enduring injury with patience and without resentment; self-control and discipline -- mastering desires and passions, especially sensual appetites. (See Galatians 5:22-23.)

- **Submission and authority:** Everyone is accountable to someone. Children are accountable to their parents' authority. Parents help their children grow and develop. Wives and husbands are subject to one another in the fear of Christ. *Wives should submit to their own husbands (Ephesians 5:21-26).* God holds the husband accountable for the proper growth and development of the family as He teaches and prepares his manservant for the work He has assigned him to do. Employees are reminded *(Titus 3:1) "to be submissive to rulers and authorities, to be obedient, to be ready for every good work."* Submission doesn't imply weakness; instead, it creates order. Order prepares us for blessing. A good leader exercises authority with wisdom and caution and knows that true leadership means to serve.

- **Servanthood:** Jesus Christ made the ultimate sacrifice. He left the highest position in heaven and took on the lowest form of creation. He gave up his Divine form to become a man. He became a servant, and He was obedient until the point of death (Philippians 2:5-11). He adopted the servant's role (John 13:4-17) to demonstrate for His disciples the principle of mutual servanthood. I encourage you to *"Let this mind be in you that was also in Christ Jesus (Philippians 2:5)."* I believe servanthood is a prerequisite for kingdom advancement. As she commits herself to service, no matter how large or small the task, the woman with a Christ-centered heart knows that God has big plans for her. She trusts God to accomplish His purpose in her life. (See Jeremiah 29:11.)

- **Influence:** This woman creates the atmosphere in her home, on her job, among friends, and with strangers. She leads her home with discipline and self-assurance. This woman exhibits the qualities of a leader. She's trustworthy, a positive influence, a hard worker, and a planner and protector of her family. Her achievements are notable -- she meets the needs of her home, she invests for her household, she keeps herself in shape, and she helps her husband become successful. Her attitude is delightful, healthy, compassionate, unselfish, and public. Her family applauds her for her works and God's word.

- **Discernment:** This woman comprehends God's design for life as expressed in *Ecclesiastes 3:1-4: "To everything there is a season, a time for every purpose under heaven: a time to be born, and a time to die; a time to plant, and a time to pluck what is planted; a time to kill, and a time to heal; a time to break down, and a time to build up; a time to weep and a time to laugh; a time to mourn and a time to dance."* The words of a woman with the heart of God speak wisdom in the life of others.

Assessment

The questions below will help you assess your Christ-centered characteristic and give you some perspective on whether Christ is at the center of your life.

Through whom are we able to produce the fruit of the spirit (Gal. 5:22)?

Do you struggle with forgiveness when someone hurts you? Why?

Are there times in your life when you feel hopeless?

Do you find that people are always asking you if something is wrong?

Is there an authority figure in your life to whom you have trouble submitting?

Are you a servant leader (do you serve the people under your authority)?

Do you possess the obedience to be a good servant?

Do you trust that God has a plan for you?

Does your presence change the atmosphere of a room upon entering (positively)?

Do you frequently regret things that you say?

Confessions

Stop here to confess any areas in your life in which you need the work of the Holy Spirit.

Write those things here:

Let's Pray

Father, without reservation, I surrender every area of my life completely to you. I confess my sins and pray that your word will purify me from all unrighteousness. Help me to keep you in the center of my life. In Jesus' name, amen.

Seeking Godly Counsel

- Always consult the word of God for direction in any area of your life.
- Set aside some time so you can commune with Christ and ask Him for counsel.
- Fellowship with other believers.
- Also check out the resources within your church -- classes, Bible study.
- Look for Christian counselors in your local church and/or community.

Recommendation

Use discernment: Make sure you confide in the right people.

Resources

- A good Bible-teaching church

- Workshops, classes, seminars, discipleship courses

- Spiritually mature women of God

- Seek out a spiritual mother

- Develop a spiritual sister

- Mentor a younger lady in her spiritual growth.

Evaluation Summary

The Holy Spirit produces fruit in our lives (Galatians 5:22-23). Because the Holy Spirit uses us as vessels for His use, you must recognize the need to forgive others as He has forgiven you. You know that unless you forgive, the Father cannot forgive you. Hopelessness and sadness could be signs that there are things in your life that cause you to become disconnected from your source of hope, for Christ is the ever-present hope.

If you believe that Christ was raised and that He is the sustainer of your hope, joy, peace, and so on, then you understand that submission is the next step toward deliverance. When we submit to God's authority in our lives, we're able to come under the authority of others. God prepares us for promotion by teaching us to serve our authorities and everyone else around us. A heart of service is a prerequisite to your next spiritual promotion.

Joseph is a perfect illustration of how God elevates those who have a heart of service. Joseph trusted in his dream even after he was hated and discarded by his brothers. He was propositioned by Potiphar's wife and later accused of assault, yet he stood fast on the promise of God. He was despised and rejected, sold into slavery, falsely accused, and imprisoned; nevertheless, his persistent state of humility allowed God to fulfill His purpose and plan for his life. Joseph had the favor of God on his life because of the characteristics that he displayed everywhere he went (servanthood, humility, Christ-centered heart, integrity, discernment).

As you review and compare your assessment with the evaluation summary above, note any areas that need improvement and work toward affirming yourself through the word of God. I encourage you to continue applying the characteristics listed in principle number one to your life. These characteristics will reveal the heartbeat of God. Align your heart with the heart of God and submit yourself as a Christ-centered vessel. Remember: Allow God to help you identify the areas that need work.

2. AFFIRMATION- AFFIRMING YOURSELF THROUGH THE WORD OF GOD

Wikipedia-encyclopedia says that affirmation is "a form of autosuggestion in which a statement of a desirable intention or condition of the world or the mind is deliberately meditated on or repeated in order to implant it in the mind." Autosuggestion is a process by which an individual trains the subconscious mind to believe something.

I remember a time in my life when it seemed like I couldn't hear from God. I prayed, I listened, I read His word, but still it appeared as though He were silent. One Sunday morning I was watching television and one of the pastors was talking about the story of David and all of his ups and down. He explained how David is the perfect example of how to encourage yourself by way of affirmation. He then read a verse from the Bible and asked that we meditate on it so that it would penetrate our minds and our hearts.

I did this for 30 days and I could feel the scripture moving me from a dry place in my life into that of rushing waters. For me, this connection to God was attainable through affirmation. The scripture wasn't new; in fact, I had read it many times before. However, it was the affirming power that took me to new depths and opened up a world of intimacy and revelation between me and the Father.

On another occasion, God gave my husband and me a scripture that he wanted us to meditate on for an entire year. It said that He would be a lamp unto our feet and a light unto our path. This scripture would affirm in our spirits that despite the obstacles (giants) that we'd come up against during that year, God would be the light that would lead us out. And so it was with David. Despite murder, adultery, and other wilderness experiences, it was his consistent affirmations of God's position in his life that drew him back to his Father. In *Psalm 91, David said, "He who dwells in the secret place of the most High shall abide under the shadow of the almighty. I will say of the Lord, He is my refuge and my fortress: my God; in him I will trust."*

Lesson: You must trust the word of God as being God-inspired.

Characteristics of a woman who affirms herself through the word of God:

- **Connected:** When a woman remains connected to the power of the Holy Spirit, she anchors herself in the word of God. This will manifest supernatural power through affirmations in every circumstance.

- **Focused (day and night):** *Joshua 1:8 reminds her to "meditate on the word day and night, observing to do all that is written in it. For then you will make your way prosperous and you will have good success."*

- **Consistent:** Just as she eats daily in order to nourish her physical body, she also must eat the bread of life from the Father's table to stay spiritually healthy. (See Luke 9:23.)

- **Diligent:** When this woman affirms herself in the word, she demonstrates tenacity. She knows that the Lord has awesome things in store for her. Proverbs 10:4 says, "He who has a slack hand becomes poor but the diligent hand makes rich."

- **Confident**: *"Being confident of this very thing, that he which hath begun a good work in you will perform it until the day of Jesus Christ." (Phil 1:6)*

181

Assessment

Do you have a consistent quiet time? How often?

Describe your secret place (where you meet with God alone daily).

When difficult situations confront you, do you see opportunities for spiritual growth?

Are you often distracted during your time with the Lord and find it hard to hear from Him?

Do you apply the word of God to every area of your life (finances, relationships, children, health, and wealth)? How?

Do you show yourself diligent in interacting with the word of God (study, read, listen, pray)?

Are you easily discouraged when the people closest to you speak negatively of you? Why?

Describe the people or things that you allow to distract you.

Do you find that you pray more or less depending on your situation?

Are you sometimes too busy to talk to God?

Confessions

Stop here to confess any areas in your life in which you need the work of the Holy Spirit.

Write those things here:

Let's Pray

Dear Father, forgive me for not affirming Your word in my heart. I desire to confirm your word consistently so that I can be careful to maintain a good work and present myself profitable unto man and to You. In Jesus' name, amen.

Seeking Godly Counsel

- Partner with faithful Christian people (fellowship).

- Seek God about finding a prayer partner, someone who will affirm the word of God through prayer.

- Find a Bible that will meet you at your specific place of development.

- Regularly attend a good, Bible-teaching church.

- Participate in Bible study.

- Become part of a ministry within your church.

Recommendation

Use discernment: Make sure you confide in the right people.

Resources

- Put these principles in practice.

- Keep your affirmations in the present tense.

- Meditate.

- Read books on affirmation.

- Use tapes, sermons, and videos that affirm the word of God.

- Attend workshops and seminars.

Evaluation Summary

Confirming the word of God in your life requires discipline to ensure your purpose and destiny here on earth. The characteristics listed above reveal the discipline you need. The woman who affirms herself with the word of God stays connected to the source (Holy Spirit) that supplies all of her needs. She is focused and relentless on her journey toward pleasing God, who desires that she bears fruit.

The Bible speaks in several places that Jesus went off to be alone with his Father. He knew the importance of spending time in order to stay focused on the purpose of His being here. It was that time with God that enabled Him to endure all that He came up against. When Satan attempted to distract and tempt Him, He made it known that the word was confirmed in Him. He was totally confident that His Father would sustain Him -- therefore he could stand.

Christ's disciples denied themselves and abandoned everything to follow Him and still He wouldn't even allow them to pull Him away from His purpose and ultimate plan. In this day and time we may feel that we're entirely too busy to spend the time that Christ did with the Heavenly Father; however, the secret to the balance we need in our lives is revealed to us through spending time with Him. As you review and compare your assessment with the evaluation summary above, note any areas that need improvement and work toward affirming yourself through the word of God. I encourage you to continue applying the characteristics listed in this principle to your life. (Remember to allow God to help you identify the areas in which you need help.)

3. CULTIVATE THE HEART OF HUMILITY

Whoever exalts himself will be humbled, and whoever humbles himself will be exalted (Matthew 23:12). The haughty looks of man shall be brought low, and the lofty pride of men shall be humbled, and the LORD alone shall be EXALTED in that day (Isaiah 2:11).

Humility is one of those characteristics that can deceive us. In today's time it's hard to tell if a person is faking it or is truly humble according to the standards of God.

First Peter 5:5 teaches the young that they should submit unto the elders and be clothed in humility, for God resists the proud and gives grace to the humble.

In my ministry I see women make this mistake over and over again. Because we're submitted vessels, often we feel that others will overlook our accomplishments. We want to show others our good works, so we strategically set up situations to win recognition and/or stand up before any audience and announce our achievements.

The Bible makes it clear that when we reward ourselves this way, this is the only reward we will receive; however, when we humble ourselves and trust God, He will reward our good works in a way that eyes have not seen and ears have not heard. The great thing is that He will do it in a way that all things will work together for His glory. Don't fret because a man/woman didn't recognize your achievements. Just wait on God. People may choose to keep you out of the game, but when God raises you up you're not only in the game but you're also the most valuable player. In other words, you're no longer the tail but you are the head. You're no longer the borrower but the lender, not beneath but above, and blessed coming and going (see Deuteronomy 28). These are just a few of your rewards for clothing yourself in the spirit of humility!

Lesson: God sees every little thing that you do, and you must trust

Him to use your gifting for His glory. When you meditate on that thought you'll know that every little thing that you do will work together for His good. Remember *Phil 2:3: "Let nothing be done through selfish ambition or conceit, but in lowliness of mind let each esteem others better than themselves."* In other words, keep wearing your garment of humility.

Some characteristics of a woman who cultivates a heart of humility:

- **Wise:** Wisdom is a valuable principle. The book of James tells us that true wisdom comes from above and is pure, then peaceable, gentle and easy to be entreated, full of mercy and good fruit, without partiality and without hypocrisy. Wisdom doesn't always come with age. We're all born with sense knowledge (taste, sight, sound, touch, and so on). The longer we depend on our sense knowledge and less on godly revelations, the longer we'll be mere infants in wisdom. A wise woman shares her wisdom with family and friends and witnesses the fruit it bears.
- **Meek:** The world has convinced us that meekness is a sign of weakness but the word of God tells us just the opposite. In

Psalm 37:11 we find that the meek shall inherit the earth and delight themselves in the abundance of peace. God can't use us if we aren't meek; indeed, this is a necessary requirement of ministry. The opposite of meek is arrogance. Arrogance is worldly and offensive.

- **Gracious:** I believe so much in the characteristics of living a gracious life that our magazine, *Beauty for Ashes*, has developed an entire outreach effort to empower, connect, and equip women with tools to live graciously. *Proverbs 11:16* lets us know that *"A gracious woman retains honor."* This woman knows her worth; therefore, she's kind, courteous, and finds comfort in her relationship with her Father.

- **Pleasant:** This woman smiles. Yes, this is simple but it's major. Her hospitality engulfs you and welcomes you into her space. She's never mean-spirited, unapproachable, or "mad at the world." Proverbs 3:17 says that her ways are ways of pleasantness, and all her paths are peace.

- **Empowering:** She is simply empowered by the filling of the Holy Spirit on a daily basis. *"Do not get drunk on wine, which leads to debauchery. Instead, be filled with the Spirit (Eph. 5:18 NIV)."*

Assessment

Name three ways that you are using the "pure" wisdom mentioned above in your life.

What are some evidences of bearing fruit in the area of wisdom?

Why do you think the world views meekness as weakness?

Describe a time when your meekness was misunderstood as weakness.

How can you equip yourself to live a more gracious life?

What are some ways you can teach others to manifest gracious characteristics?

Explain how you view the value of a smile.

How do you prepare yourself daily to be pleasant?

List reasons why you always need a mentor, a "mentee," and a Christian peer.

How can you empower yourself?

Confessions

Stop here to confess any areas in your life in which you need the work of the Holy Spirit.

Write those things here:

Let's Pray

Heavenly Father, I ask for forgiveness for getting ahead of you and trying to direct my own destiny. Please give me wisdom and teach me to cultivate a heart of humility. In Jesus' name, amen.

Seeking Godly Counsel

- Stay connected to faithful Christian people (fellowship).
- Regularly attend a good, Bible-teaching church.
- Participate in Bible study.
- Become a part of a serving ministry within your church.
- Seek counsel from an older, godly woman, find a godly peer to

fellowship with, and identify a young lady with whom you can share God's wisdom.

Recommendation

Use discernment: Make sure you confide in the right people.

Resources

- Books on humility
- Identify and learn from a person who exemplifies humility
- Study the many ways that Christ showed humility
- Attend workshops and seminars

Evaluation Summary

Solomon was the wisest man in the Bible. The Bible reveals numerous accounts about the wisdom in his life; however, you must understand that Solomon asked for wisdom. James 1:5 tells us that if we lack wisdom we can ask God for it and He will give it to us liberally and without reproach.

One of the keys to activating the power of pure wisdom in your life is by asking the Father. This wisdom from above, as mentioned in James 3:17, reveals itself through peace, gentleness, mercy, and good fruit. It's not prejudiced nor is it hypocritical. In order to do these things, we must exemplify a heart of meekness. Matthew 5:5 reveals the secret: God blesses those who are meek, and they will inherit the earth. Remember, the evil one doesn't want you to inherit the earth, so he invites you to participate in his confusion so that he can steal your inheritance.

When you realize his tricks and you align yourself with your inheritance from your Heavenly Father, you'll equip yourself to live graciously. As you equip yourself to live a gracious life, you'll know that helping others develop characteristics of a gracious life is a part of your growth and development. When I meet a woman for the first time who greets me with a smile, I know that she knows something about living a gracious life. Her smile entreats me to listen to her. Her positive words empower others. Her value immediately increases through her smile; therefore, one of the easiest ways to prepare yourself to be pleasant is to look in the mirror before leaving home and give yourself a big smile.

Sometimes a smile is a beautiful way to enlarge your territory to make room for more blessing in your life. When you allow God to expand your territory He puts mentors, mentees, and gracious friends in your life for the purpose of bearing fruit.

As you review and compare your assessment with the evaluation summary above, note any areas that need improvement and work toward strengthening your desire through the word of God to clothe yourself in humility. I encourage you to continue applying the characteristics listed in this principle to your life. These characteristics will give you an appetite for humility and teach you how to live graciously. (Remember to allow God to help you identify the areas in which you need help.)

4. INTERCEDE FOR OTHERS IN PRAYER

To intercede on behalf of others means to pray and petition for someone else's breakthrough. This is another one of those "secrets" that so many of us miss.

The story of Job is an excellent example of how we can attain deliverance by praying for others. *Job 42:10 says, "And the LORD turned the captivity of Job, when he prayed for his friends: also the*

LORD gave Job twice as much as he had before." Not only did he receive his breakthrough, but the Lord gave him double for his trouble.

Occasionally a young woman will come to me for spiritual guidance. As we unfold the issues that threaten to consume her, we find that she's done everything that she knows to do. This includes praying for the situation, reading relative scriptures, listening to relative teachings, and requesting prayer from other believers. These are all necessary ways to seek deliverance. Sometimes, however, we won't see the hand of God until we take the focus off of our own needs and put it on the needs of others. When we redirect our attention to someone who may be in a similar situation, we release our issues to God, thus allowing Him to show Himself.

Lesson: Prayer changes you and your focus! Sometimes when we focus on our situation, we get caught up in our issues and don't allow the word of God to frame or focus our prayers. When we take our eyes off of ourselves, we allow God to deliver us.

Characteristics of a woman who intercedes for others in prayer:

- **Connected:** Christ says that if we stay connected to Him then we'll bear much fruit. Apart from Him we can do nothing. He promises that if we abide in Him and His word abides in us, then we can ask whatever we wish and it will be given to us (John 15:5-7). An intercessor knows that outside of the vine she has no life... no power.

- **Aware:** She's aware of the power of the gift of petitioning on another's behalf. She understands that God is using her; therefore, she models her life according to the teachings of the word. James 5:16 says that we're to pray for one another that we might be healed. The effective, fervent prayer of a righteous man/woman avails much.

- **Courageous:** This woman has a boldness and strong belief that God will answer her prayer. She has the fortitude that enables her to wait patiently on the Lord. *Psalm 27:14 says it best: "Wait on the LORD: be of good courage, and he shall strengthen thine heart."*

- **Disciplined:** To think about others in the midst of personal struggles requires discipline. This woman acquires discipline through obedience to the Holy Spirit. When she obeys the Holy Spirit, He positions her to intercede on behalf of others.

- **Committed:** When a woman commits herself to God, she shows herself faithful and dependable in the army of the Lord. She dresses for success. She has her helmet of salvation, she girds herself with truth, and she carries her sword of the spirit and the shield of faith. She shods her feet with the preparation of the gospel of peace and wears the breastplate of righteousness, praying always with all prayer and supplication in the spirit (Eph. 6:11-18). She is ready and committed to the cause.

Assessment

In what ways do you maintain your connection with God?

Do you struggle with going to God on behalf of others?

Name situations or an instance when you prayed for someone else without that person asking for prayer.

Has the Holy Spirit nudged you to pray for someone you don't know or a situation of which you are unaware?

Name a time when you were at your lowest point and somehow found the strength to intercede for someone else.

Explain how God has used you to pray for your foe.

Discipline gives you the maturity and consistency to enter into the presence of God. How did you acquire this discipline?

Some say that obedience is the key to opening the window of heaven. How has God blessed you through your obedience to intercede on behalf of others?

What burden caused you to intercede for others?

Are you committed to pray for others around you as needed? Why?

Confessions

Stop here to confess any areas in your life in which you need the work of the Holy Spirit.

Write those things here:

Let's Pray

Lord God, forgive me for the times that I haven't interceded on the behalf of others. Holy Spirit, increase in me that I may be sensitive to you in order to discern the need to pray for those who you send in my circle of influence. In Jesus' name, amen.

Seeking Godly Counsel

- Psalms 1:1-3
- Your pastor
- Youth pastor
- Church counselors
- Scripture
- His promises
- The Holy Spirit
- Devotionals
- Advisors
- Parents
- Wise men and women

Recommendation

Use discernment: Make sure you confide in the right people.

Resources

- John 8:32

- Become a part of a ministry of intercessory prayer.

- Read books on prayer.

- Attend prayer workshops.

- Find a prayer partner.

- Seek out prayer groups.

- Learn about prayer, intercession, and petitions.

Evaluation Summary

We can connect to the Holy Spirit in many ways; however, we recommend that you maintain a daily quiet time that includes reading His word, praying in faith, and listening for His voice.

One of the secrets to our blessings lies within the process of bearing fruit or making disciples. In order to do that we must intercede for others and pray with others. I can remember on occasions when I would pass an accident or see something on the news. I'd hear a voice telling me that I should take a minute to pray for that person or the situation. My lowest point was when I lost my only son. The pain that I saw my mother go through as a result of losing her only grandchild caused me to forget about my own heartache and to focus on helping her to get through.

God taught me a long time ago that if I pray for my enemies, He would align their lives with His will and His word in whatever situation. The more you're in the presence of God, the more you desire to be in His presence. This maturing process gives you the discipline that sustains your spiritual consistency. The Bible says that obedience is far better than sacrifice (1 Samuel 15:22). When we obey the Holy Spirit concerning intercession, we put ourselves in the pathway of blessings.

As you review and compare your assessment with the evaluation summary above, note any areas that need improvement and work toward strengthening your desire through the word of God to intercede for others. I encourage you to continue applying the characteristics listed in this principle to your life.

5. ENCOURAGEMENT

I was talking to a friend who shared with me an eye-opening experience. She was trying to stop smoking and wasn't as successful as she would have liked. Around 2 a.m. she awoke with a coughing spell. Within three minutes it was gone. She went to work the next day and came back home that evening.

The same coughing spell awakened her again. This time her husband made her go to the ER. Doctors gave her a chest X-ray but everything was fine. The next morning around 2 a.m. , she was awakened again with coughing and vomiting. She went to another emergency care clinic and returned home with an allergy prescription and recommendations to relax.

The next night the coughing was so excruciating that she began to cough up blood. Her family agreed that she would have to see a specialist, even though it was outside of her insurance plan.

The doctor checked her and found that a violent cancer was quickly spreading throughout her body, starting with her respiratory system. She needed radiation therapy and possibly chemo immediately. She was fighting for her life.

She went home after the diagnosis, but no one told her about the

MAKE YOUR MOUTH A MINISTRY: *Speak Life ...*

deep black hole that she would soon fall into after receiving such devastating news. She was suicidal and her family was on 24-hour watch, afraid for her life. The doctor prescribed antidepressants. She didn't see how she would come through this. This was her secret:

She was addicted to the same drug from which she helped others find freedom ever day. Further, many people around her didn't know about her depression or the reason for her cancer.

But there was a Friend who did know. Jesus knew everything and He taught her to encourage herself.

Through this experience she came to know Jesus in a way that she never had before. She now seeks to go deeper into His presence. Not only is she now cancer-free, but she also learned to encourage herself in God's word.

Lesson: Sometimes encouragement can heal people. Encouragement increases their self-esteem and deepens their relationship with Christ.

Characteristics of a woman who knows how to encourage herself:

- **Optimistic:** This woman walks in anticipation; she sees the silver lining in every cloud. She sees growth and success, not failure. She looks up and not down; she speaks life and not death. She believes Psalm 18:30, that "This God—his way is perfect; the word of the Lord proves true; he is a shield for all those who take refuge in him." The book of Ruth is a great read to strengthen your encouragement muscles.

- **Surrendered:** She has surrendered all unto God, and she honestly knows that all of her help comes from Him. She trusts Him with her whole heart. She speaks with confidence before the storm is over as a way of encouraging herself. *"So if there is any encouragement in Christ, any comfort from love, any participation in the Spirit, any affection and sympathy, complete my joy by being of the same mind, having the same love, being in full accord and of one mind (Philippians 2:1-2)."*

- **Personable:** When you speak it appears that you have her undivided attention. She listens attentively. She never makes you feel that she's tired of engaging with you, even if she is--which leaves you in a state of encouragement. She knows that *"every* *person should be quick to hear, slow to speak, slow to anger; for the anger of a person does not produce the righteousness that God requires (James 1:19-20)."* She also realizes, *"God will bring every work into judgment, including every secret thing, whether it is good or whether it is evil (Ecclesiastes12: 14)."*

- **Enthusiastic:** You can tell if this person is in the room. People who are enthusiastic about what they do show it naturally. She's passionate and dedicated. She inspires you with her infectious spirit and motivates you to want to do more. Romans 12:11 remind us, *"Do not be slothful in zeal, be fervent (enthusiastic) in spirit, serving the Lord."*

- **Assurance:** The assured woman has qualities of wholeness that lead to responsible living. She has a proper understanding of God's power, so she encourages repenting and uncertain believers to call upon God for deliverance and walk securely in His love. This attitude of trust in God removes the presumptive pride of the woman who trusts her own good works for salvation, or the agonizing doubt of the believer who's sensitive to her own transgression. *The assured woman will be confident (assured) in His presence (I John 3:19).*

Assessment

Define encouragement.

What's the best way to encourage someone who needs a friend?

Describe a time when someone discouraged you.

How did this affect your perspective on that situation?

List words of discouragement and then list words of encouragement that counteract the negative words.

Ask some of the people closest to you if they consider you an encourager or a discourager.

Explain what they said to you and why.

Do you think this is an accurate reflection of how you see yourself?

What is your Christian responsibility concerning encouragement?

Recall a few examples of a person encouraging himself or herself that you would want to imitate.

Confessions

Stop here to confess any areas in your life in which you need the work of the Holy Spirit.

Write those things here:

Let's Pray

Lord, forgive me for failing to be an encouraging instrument used for your glory. Teach me the characteristics of an encourager and let your ways show through me daily. In Jesus' name, amen.

Seeking Godly Counsel

- Your pastor
- Youth pastor
- Church counselors
- Scripture
- His promises
- The Holy Spirit
- Devotionals
- Advisors
- Parents
- Wise men and women

Recommendation

Use discernment: Make sure you confide in the right people.

Resources

- Sing praises to God

- Christian fellowship

- Stories in the Bible that encourage the saints

- Affirm yourself in the Lord

- Sign up for encouragement workshops

- Read books on encouragement

Evaluation Summary

Praise is one way to encourage one another and stimulate/create an atmosphere of joy and hope. Encouragement gives hope, confidence, or courage. Sometimes our circumstances create a spirit of discouragement. When these situations occur, you need to know how to empower yourself.

Pour God's word into your spirit. Affirm yourself by finding out what God says about you. Words of encouragement are always words full of life. Recognize that discouragement is a trick of the enemy to steal your joy. If you find that what you have to say to others often isn't uplifting or inspiring, begin to transform your state of mind (attitude) so that you view the world around you as God has intended -- as a gift.

We're exposed to negativity on a daily basis; indeed, it's all around us. This is why, as Christians, we must bring light to these otherwise dark situations. It's our responsibility to uplift and encourage even when we ourselves are discouraged.

6. Speaking the Truth in Love

My husband and I often take courses that teach us the art of preaching; in other words, how to become better preachers. In these courses we learn the different types and styles of preaching. We also have an opportunity, along with other classmates, to prepare and present sermons that illustrate a particular style of preaching.

Preparing to preach requires a lot of work. As we get closer to the date we're to preach, we have books, articles, and research all over the place. We even practice by preaching our sermons to each other and asking for true feedback. When my husband would preach his sermons to me, I would take detailed notes, tell him how I felt, and highlight the areas that I thought needed improvement. I was certain that I was helping him. However, before I could finish my feedback he was upset, dejected, discouraged, and never wanted to preach to me again.

It was obvious he didn't like what I was saying and I really couldn't understand what I had done wrong. I would say to myself, "He is too sensitive and he doesn't understand that if I don't tell him the world will tell him." I DON'T WANT YOU TO MISS THIS BECAUSE THIS IS THE MOST IMPORTANT THING I GIVE IN THIS BOOK.   Love is the "glue " that holds everything together. Paul tells us in Colossians 2:2 that we should be knitted together in love, Ephesians 3:17 says that we should be "rooted and grounded" in love. In my preaching experience with my husband that I talked about above, it's clear that something was missing -- love.

Be mindful of the wisdom in *Proverbs 12:25: "Anxiety in the heart of a person causes depression, but a good word makes it glad."* When I gave my husband feedback on his preaching, it was the truth as I saw it. However, we know that God is Love, so truth without God's love is not truth. My husband responded that way because the love was missing. I blamed it on his oversensitivity, even though I was completely unaware of the lack of love that showed in my tone and speech.

Truthfully, I didn't even think of God being the teacher and allowing

Him to use me to give my husband the feedback that He wanted my husband to have. I told my husband what I thought and felt like he should make the adjustments accordingly. It is so much bigger than that. Jesus Christ is the greatest teacher who ever lived. What was I thinking? I don't know -- but I don't want you to make the same mistake.

The Lesson: Whenever you give any type of feedback to others, the other person must see the love in the feedback; otherwise, you'll open the door for Satan to plant thoughts of envy, strife, contention, and insincerity in the mind of the other person. Because you've accepted Jesus Christ as your Savior, you must lace your truth in love.

Characteristics of a woman who speaks the truth in love:

- **Called/Chosen:** God has called her to speak truth in love to you. *God's divine power has granted to us all things that pertain to life and godliness, through the knowledge of Him who called us to his own glory and excellence (2 Peter 1:3). As God's chosen one, He has put on her compassion, kindness, humility, meekness, and patience so that she may speak truth in love (Colossians 3:12).*

- **Maturity:** The mark of a mature woman is that she eats solid food and has the power of discernment trained by constant practice to distinguish "good" from "evil" (Hebrews 5:14). She acknowledges with great triumph: *"When I was a child, I spoke as a child, I understood as a child, I thought as a child: but when I became a mature (woman), I put away childish things (I Corinthians 13:11)."*

- **Powerful:** This woman might have high status on the basis of significant personal capacity, but she must know the scriptures and the power of God. She also must recognize that even if she has *"prophetic powers, and understand all mysteries and all knowledge, and if she has all faith, so as to remove mountains, she must speak love, or she is nothing (I Corinthians 13:2 – paraphrased)."*

- **Accessible:** The accessible woman is qualified and willing to assume responsibility of speaking to and on behalf of those in her charge. She takes seriously the saying in *Zechariah 3:7: "Thus says the Lord of hosts: If you will walk in my ways and keep my charge, then you shall rule my house and have charge of my courts, and I will give you the right of access among those who are standing here."*

- **Benevolent:** Living under grace, she lives a life of love and service, always willing to do good *"as unto the Lord, and not to men (Ephesians 6:7)."*

Assessment

When you must tell someone something that you know will cause hurt feelings, how do you prepare yourself to tell the person the truth?

Will you be there to pick up the pieces after you've shared your truth with a friend?

When do you feel that you have the authority to tell people about themselves?

Do you have friends who seem to demand that you walk on egg-shells in order to protect their feelings? Why or why not?

Should your friends have to accept your words because of who you are to them? Why or why not?

Before you speak do you consider how your words will affect the other person?

Do you feel that you are a part of the solution or the problem when you tell your truth? Why or why not?

If you know the truth about a situation and you haven't been asked to share, do you feel you must tell what you know? Why or why not?

What was the worst thing that ever happened when you shared a truth that wasn't received in love?

How do you help to heal the wounds of your words?

Confessions

Stop here to confess any areas in your life in which you need the work of the Holy Spirit.

Write those things here:

Let's Pray

Lord, forgive me for failing to be your truth to the people you've assigned me to speak into for your glory. Teach me the characteristics of a person who speaks the truth in love daily. In Jesus' name, amen.

Seeking Godly Counsel

- Your pastor
- Youth pastor
- Church counselors
- Scripture
- His promises
- The Holy Spirit
- Devotionals
- Advisors
- Parents
- Wise men and women

Recommendation

Use discernment: Make sure you confide in the right people.

Resources

- Make a decision to grow spiritually

- Affirmations

- Build relationships

- Get your orders from God before you speak

Evaluation Summary

It takes a lot of spiritual maturity to tell someone a truth that you know will hurt his or her feelings. I have learned to take that truth to prayer before I present it. Why? Because I need my heavenly Father to go before me and prepare the person as He prepares me.

Everyone struggles with this because our flesh makes us believe that our truth is what the person needs to hear, not understanding that only God's love can prepare you to speak in another's person life. You have no authority without Him. When you have to walk on eggshells to communicate with a friend, as a child of God you must allow God to speak through you.

The goal for Christians is restoration, one of the most important doctrines in the Bible. One of my pastors in my past shared with me that when God allows you to know something it doesn't mean that He has assigned you the job to tell it. Wait on the Lord and peace and restoration will occur. Man's Truth is sometimes hard to swallow. I know that in my own personal life, there have been times when I've been confronted with TRUTH, and I didn't like it. However, many times I've experienced conviction because God had already shown me, and that person's assignment was to confirm that truth for me.

A Weekly
Life Speaking Journal

MAKE YOUR MOUTH A MINISTRY
Speak Life...

52-Week Journal

Here, in this journal, you can be honest with yourself and God about your words and the state of your heart. Do your words reflect a Christ-centered heart? Are you affirming yourself and encouraging others? Are you speaking the truth in love?

During the next 52 weeks, use this journal to record your experiences and practice what you're learning as you strengthen the latent power in your mouth. For example, you can use this journal to practice turning negative comments into words that speak life! Here are a few examples:

NEGATIVE WORDS	POSITIVE WORDS
I can't wait for this day to be over!	This is the day that the Lord has made, I will be glad and I will rejoice in it.
I can't believe that you are so stupid!	You need a little more practice in this area. Let me show you how I would do it.
Why do I always have to do her job?	Lord, I know you have a blessing in this for me.

Speak Life Journal
Week #1

Negative Words	Positive Words
(I WANTED TO SAY...)	(I SAID...)
(I SAID...)	(NEXT TIME I WILL SAY...)

Speak Life Journal
Week #2

Negative Words
(I WANTED TO SAY...)
(I SAID...)

Positive Words
(I SAID...)
(NEXT TIME I WILL SAY...)

Speak Life Journal
Week #3

Negative Words	Positive Words
(I WANTED TO SAY...)	(I SAID...)
(I SAID...)	(NEXT TIME I WILL SAY...)

Speak Life Journal
Week #4

Negative Words (I WANTED TO SAY...) (I SAID...)	Positive Words (I SAID...) (NEXT TIME I WILL SAY...)

Speak Life Journal
Week #5

Negative Words
(I WANTED TO SAY...)
(I SAID...)

Positive Words
(I SAID...)
(NEXT TIME I WILL SAY...)

Speak Life Journal
Week #6

Negative Words (I WANTED TO SAY...) (I SAID...)	Positive Words (I SAID...) (NEXT TIME I WILL SAY...)

Speak Life Journal
Week #7

Negative Words	Positive Words
(I WANTED TO SAY...)	(I SAID...)
(I SAID...)	(NEXT TIME I WILL SAY...)

Speak Life Journal
Week #8

Negative Words (I WANTED TO SAY...) (I SAID...)	Positive Words (I SAID...) (NEXT TIME I WILL SAY...)

Speak Life Journal
Week #9

Negative Words (I WANTED TO SAY...) (I SAID...)	Positive Words (I SAID...) (NEXT TIME I WILL SAY...)

Speak Life Journal
Week #10

Negative Words (I WANTED TO SAY...) (I SAID...)	Positive Words (I SAID...) (NEXT TIME I WILL SAY...)

Speak Life Journal
Week #11

Negative Words
(I WANTED TO SAY...)
(I SAID...)

Positive Words
(I SAID...)
(NEXT TIME I WILL SAY...)

Speak Life Journal
Week #12

Negative Words (I WANTED TO SAY...) (I SAID...)	Positive Words (I SAID...) (NEXT TIME I WILL SAY...)

Speak Life Journal
Week #13

Negative Words	Positive Words
(I WANTED TO SAY...)	(I SAID...)
(I SAID...)	(NEXT TIME I WILL SAY...)

Speak Life Journal
Week #14

Negative Words
(I WANTED TO SAY...)
(I SAID...)

Positive Words
(I SAID...)
(NEXT TIME I WILL SAY...)

Speak Life Journal
Week #15

Negative Words
(I WANTED TO SAY...)
(I SAID...)

Positive Words
(I SAID...)
(NEXT TIME I WILL SAY...)

Speak Life Journal
Week #16

Negative Words
(I WANTED TO SAY...)
(I SAID...)

Positive Words
(I SAID...)
(NEXT TIME I WILL SAY...)

Speak Life Journal
Week #17

Negative Words (I WANTED TO SAY...) (I SAID...)	Positive Words (I SAID...) (NEXT TIME I WILL SAY...)

Speak Life Journal
Week #18

Negative Words	Positive Words
(I WANTED TO SAY...)	(I SAID...)
(I SAID...)	(NEXT TIME I WILL SAY...)

Speak Life Journal
Week #19

Negative Words (I WANTED TO SAY...) (I SAID...)	Positive Words (I SAID...) (NEXT TIME I WILL SAY...)

Speak Life Journal
Week #20

Negative Words
(I WANTED TO SAY...)
(I SAID...)

Positive Words
(I SAID...)
(NEXT TIME I WILL SAY...)

Speak Life Journal
Week #21

Negative Words	Positive Words
(I WANTED TO SAY...)	(I SAID...)
(I SAID...)	(NEXT TIME I WILL SAY...)

Speak Life Journal
Week #22

Negative Words	Positive Words
(I WANTED TO SAY...)	(I SAID...)
(I SAID...)	(NEXT TIME I WILL SAY...)

Speak Life Journal
Week #23

Negative Words
(I WANTED TO SAY...)
(I SAID...)

Positive Words
(I SAID...)
(NEXT TIME I WILL SAY...)

Speak Life Journal
Week #24

Negative Words
(I WANTED TO SAY...)
(I SAID...)

Positive Words
(I SAID...)
(NEXT TIME I WILL SAY...)

Speak Life Journal
Week #25

Negative Words
(I WANTED TO SAY...)
(I SAID...)

Positive Words
(I SAID...)
(NEXT TIME I WILL SAY...)

Speak Life Journal
Week #26

Negative Words
(I WANTED TO SAY...)
(I SAID...)

Positive Words
(I SAID...)
(NEXT TIME I WILL SAY...)

Speak Life Journal
Week #27

Negative Words (I WANTED TO SAY...) (I SAID...)	Positive Words (I SAID...) (NEXT TIME I WILL SAY...)

Speak Life Journal
Week #28

Negative Words
(I WANTED TO SAY...)
(I SAID...)

Positive Words
(I SAID...)
(NEXT TIME I WILL SAY...)

Speak Life Journal
Week #29

Negative Words
(I WANTED TO SAY...)
(I SAID...)

Positive Words
(I SAID...)
(NEXT TIME I WILL SAY...)

Speak Life Journal
Week #30

Negative Words
(I WANTED TO SAY...)
(I SAID...)

Positive Words
(I SAID...)
(NEXT TIME I WILL SAY...)

Speak Life Journal
Week #31

Negative Words
(I WANTED TO SAY...)
(I SAID...)

Positive Words
(I SAID...)
(NEXT TIME I WILL SAY...)

Speak Life Journal
Week #32

Negative Words (I WANTED TO SAY...) (I SAID...)	Positive Words (I SAID...) (NEXT TIME I WILL SAY...)

Speak Life Journal
Week #33

Negative Words (I WANTED TO SAY...) (I SAID...)	Positive Words (I SAID...) (NEXT TIME I WILL SAY...)

Speak Life Journal
Week #34

Negative Words	Positive Words
(I WANTED TO SAY...)	(I SAID...)
(I SAID...)	(NEXT TIME I WILL SAY...)

Speak Life Journal
Week #35

Negative Words
(I WANTED TO SAY...)
(I SAID...)

Positive Words
(I SAID...)
(NEXT TIME I WILL SAY...)

Speak Life Journal
Week #36

Negative Words
(I WANTED TO SAY...)
(I SAID...)

Positive Words
(I SAID...)
(NEXT TIME I WILL SAY...)

Speak Life Journal
Week #37

Negative Words
(I WANTED TO SAY...)
(I SAID...)

Positive Words
(I SAID...)
(NEXT TIME I WILL SAY...)

Speak Life Journal
Week #38

Negative Words (I WANTED TO SAY...) (I SAID...)	Positive Words (I SAID...) (NEXT TIME I WILL SAY...)

Speak Life Journal
Week #39

Negative Words
(I WANTED TO SAY...)
(I SAID...)

Positive Words
(I SAID...)
(NEXT TIME I WILL SAY...)

Speak Life Journal
Week #40

Negative Words
(I WANTED TO SAY...)
(I SAID...)

Positive Words
(I SAID...)
(NEXT TIME I WILL SAY...)

Speak Life Journal
Week #41

Negative Words (I WANTED TO SAY...) (I SAID...)	Positive Words (I SAID...) (NEXT TIME I WILL SAY...)

Speak Life Journal
Week #42

Negative Words
(I WANTED TO SAY...)
(I SAID...)

Positive Words
(I SAID...)
(NEXT TIME I WILL SAY...)

Speak Life Journal
Week #43

Negative Words
(I WANTED TO SAY...)
(I SAID...)

Positive Words
(I SAID...)
(NEXT TIME I WILL SAY...)

Speak Life Journal
Week #44

Negative Words
(I WANTED TO SAY...)
(I SAID...)

Positive Words
(I SAID...)
(NEXT TIME I WILL SAY...)

Speak Life Journal
Week #45

Negative Words (I WANTED TO SAY...) (I SAID...)	Positive Words (I SAID...) (NEXT TIME I WILL SAY...)

Speak Life Journal
Week #46

Negative Words
(I WANTED TO SAY...)
(I SAID...)

Positive Words
(I SAID...)
(NEXT TIME I WILL SAY...)

Speak Life Journal
Week #47

Negative Words
(I WANTED TO SAY...)
(I SAID...)

Positive Words
(I SAID...)
(NEXT TIME I WILL SAY...)

Speak Life Journal
Week #48

Negative Words
(I WANTED TO SAY...)
(I SAID...)

Positive Words
(I SAID...)
(NEXT TIME I WILL SAY...)

Speak Life Journal
Week #49

Negative Words
(I WANTED TO SAY...)
(I SAID...)

Positive Words
(I SAID...)
(NEXT TIME I WILL SAY...)

Speak Life Journal
Week #50

Negative Words	Positive Words
(I WANTED TO SAY...)	(I SAID...)
(I SAID...)	(NEXT TIME I WILL SAY...)

Speak Life Journal
Week #51

Negative Words
(I WANTED TO SAY...)
(I SAID...)

Positive Words
(I SAID...)
(NEXT TIME I WILL SAY...)

Speak Life Journal
Week #52

Negative Words	Positive Words
(I WANTED TO SAY...)	(I SAID...)
(I SAID...)	(NEXT TIME I WILL SAY...)

Speak Life Journal

Speak Life Journal

Speak Life Journal

Speak Life Journal

Speak Life Journal

Speak Life Journal

Speak Life Journal

Speak Life Journal

Speak Life Journal

Speak Life Journal

Speak Life Journal

Speak Life Journal

Speak Life Journal

Speak Life Journal

Speak Life Journal

Speak Life Journal

Speak Life Journal

Speak Life Journal

Speak Life Journal

About the Author

Deborah Leaner is a dynamic, energizing, motivational speaker, preacher, and spiritual life coach. She is the founder and chief executive officer of Deborah Leaner Ministries (DLM). The mission of DLM is to equip, restore, and transform women through the word of God. In 2003, Mrs. Leaner also founded Divine Discipleship for Sisters, a discipleship ministry for women.

In 2004, she co-authored a four-book series entitled "New in Him Every Day," designed to help individuals develop a deeper level of intimacy with Christ by "Knowing Who You Are in Christ," "The Power of Prayer," "Spiritual Warfare," and "One-on-One Evangelism Through Journaling." After five years of serving women from various churches in the Washington, DC, metro area, Divine Discipleship for Sisters will continue to serve women ministry leaders through churches nationwide by training women ministry leaders or the pastor's designee to disciple their women.

Mrs. Leaner is married to Deacon Tony Leaner. Together they serve in ministry at their church, First Baptist Church of Glenarden, under the pastoral leadership of John K. Jenkins, Sr.

The Leaners founded the Korey "Alex" Leaner Foundation after the loss of their son in 2005. The foundation provides one-on-one and group mentoring and life-skills training for at-risk youth.

More Resources from Deborah Leaner

Beauty for Ashes -- More Than a Magazine!

Beauty for Ashes furthers Deborah Leaner's vision to equip, restore, and transform lives for the Master's use. This e-zine serves a diverse audience of believers and nonbelievers in the community one person at a time, one community at a time, through a multi-media, holistic approach.

Taking Women's Ministries to Another Level

After five years of serving women from various churches in the Washington, DC, metro area, Divine Discipleship for Sisters will continue to serve women ministry leaders through churches nationwide by training women ministry leaders or the pastor's designee to disciple their women. The 16-hour program will impart knowledge to those who want to grow their women's ministries and help women equip, restore, and transform their lives.

Everyone who attends the workshop will receive a Certificate of Completion.

For more information, call (301) 505-1546.

Check It All Out at
www.DeborahLeaner.com

Visit this dynamic site today to learn more about Make Your Mouth A Ministry, the Tea Room, Beauty for Ashes, upcoming events, and much more!